Bristol in the Fifties

MUDDLING THROUGH
BRISTOL IN THE FIFTIES

As remembered by:

James Belsey · Michael Jenner · Roger Bennett
Helen Reid · Michael Cocks · Derek Robinson
David Foot · Alston Thomas

REDCLIFFE
Bristol

First published in 1988
by Redcliffe Press Ltd., 49 Park St., Bristol

ISBN 0 948265 97 3

Typeset and printed in Great Britain by
Penwell Ltd., Parkwood, Callington, Cornwall

Contents

The authors wish to thank Bristol United Press librarian Jerry Brooke and photographer Martin Chainey for their assistance in the selection and preparation of the photographs.

The Authors

James Belsey
Writer and
Evening Post
journalist

Roger Bennett
Broadcaster, writer
and jazz man

Michael Cocks
Former Bristol
MP, government
chief whip and
now Lord Cocks
of Hartcliffe

David Foot
Freelance writer
and Guardian
correspondent on
sport and theatre

Michael Jenner
Architect, writer
and broadcaster

Helen Reid
Writer and
Western Daily
Press *journalist*

Derek Robinson
Award winning
novelist and writer

Alston Thomas
Bristol's best
known post-war
showbiz writer

Introduction

It was a long, long journey from Clement Attlee and post-war austerity to Harold Macmillan and Supermac prosperity, just as long as the bumpy ride from Vera Lynn and the well-disciplined big bands to such 'subversive', 'corruptive' sounds as cellar jazz and rock 'n' roll. In between lay 15 years of rebuilding—morale as well as homes and factories—re-thinking and change. That is what we're looking at in this book, the changes seen through the eyes of eight writers.

It is all too easy to forget what Bristol looked like in those days. The map and the skyline of the city have altered so drastically that the street scenes come as a shock 30 or more years later.

I saw Bristol for the first time right at the start of the 1950s. We drove down the Bath Road, past the Three Lamps junction and my heart sank. Even today this is one of the drabbest entrances to an attractive city that I know, but at the turn of the 1950s it was a wretched view. Before me lay a wasteland of empty sites and poster hoardings, rust coloured buildings and grimy railway yards. It was a hot, late afternoon in July and the afternoon sunshine, never kind to cities at the best of times, made Bristol look a miserable place. I knew all about bomb sites and the gloom they cast on cityscapes—we lived in central London and I was well used to the pitiful spectacle of buildings torn and smashed, of crazy patchworks of wallpaper and broken fireplaces left madly suspended up open walls, of buddleia sprouting from the corpses of what had once been homes or shops or public buildings. But I'd seen nothing quite as bad as the old centre of Bristol.

Later I saw Clifton and the gloom deepened. It smelt of decay and despondency and had an eerie, haunted atmosphere. Old people peered through grimy lace curtains and the rusty iron balconies of the Regency and Georgian terraces looked so fragile that it seemed the slightest touch would reduce them to powder. The tall houses were blistered and cracked and covered with peeling paint which flaked down to the basements and pavements below.

Bristol had had a hard war. Coventry won the headlines and sympathy, London was as self-obsessed with its war wounds as ever but Bristol's agony had been disguised by an off-hand anonymity. It was blitzed at a time when newspapers were forbidden by the censors to name areas of destruction, so the Bristol ordeal happened in a city "in the south west", the nation heard. The nation forgot and Bristolians were robbed of their rightful place in the story of the war. Yet, in truth, Bristol suffered the most devastating, concentrated air attacks seen in Britain and its ancient centre, around the axis of the Castle Street/Wine Street area, was blasted away. It was a wound from which the city still suffers almost half a century later. The blitz shook morale badly and confidential reports spoke primly and disapprovingly of a loss of spirit in the city.

When peace came, the war had left a monumental task of reconstruction. Things didn't begin as badly as people feared. For a start, there wasn't the mass unemployment and disillusion that had followed the First World War.

The better Bristol employers had kept open jobs for employees who had been called away to the Services, but the gesture wasn't necessary. There was lots to do.

The 1945 General Election saw the great war leader Winston Churchill soundly defeated—enough of that Churchillian bellicosity, thank you, it was time for Peace—and the ascetic, idealist, socialist Clement Attlee returned in his place by a country which wanted to build a better, more decent Britain. And that's just what a lot of people tried to do, with varying degrees of success and failure.

What followed in the years between Attlee's hopes and ideals and the jaunty bounty of an increasingly prosperous Britain under Harold Macmillan—it matters not a whit whether he actually said "You've never had it so good", he *meant* it—is the background to this book. This is not, definitely not, any kind of attempt to record a formal history of Bristol in the post-war years but it is a stab at recalling the flavour of the period and what these years meant to us.

We have the wisdom of hindsight, of course. Those years saw some dreadful mistakes in Bristol and it isn't difficult to spot them from the vantage point of several decades later. Mike Jenner takes a typically acerbic look at the way planners and architects deal with the city in the great post-war building boom. It's also curious to see, thanks to Michael—now Lord—Cocks, how the post-war Bristol politicians maintained close personal friendships across the political divide, one of the brighter legacies of the war with its coalition approach.

Roger Bennett remembers the rise and rise of jazz and Alston Thomas, who pounded the showbiz beat in Bristol during these years, can remember a kaleidescope of arts and entertainment, from Sir Thomas Beecham demanding a new Colston Hall to Tony Hancock at the Hippodrome. Derek Robinson takes a wry look at his youth in a Bristol still a long, long way from the liberal revolution of the 1960s and Helen Reid recalls her salad days as an undergraduate at Bristol University in the 50s. I kept Brabazon for myself because I loved her as a schoolboy and I still love her after all these years, and David Foot looks back to a colourful chapter of sporting history as old heroes like Wally Hammond made their final bows and new heroes made their entrances.

The Cold War came and stayed, the Korean War came and went, Suez and its aftermath bitterly divided the country and we grew to accept that the nuclear age had truly arrived. That was the international scene. In Bristol, people muddled through, made changes, tried to clear up the mess of war and from the cold, hard reality of rationing and austerity grew the first little flowers of prosperity as the 50s ended in the brilliant summer of 1959 and the beautiful autumn that followed it.

It Was Different Then!

How Derek Robinson discovered life in the
Fifties

Miss Watkins had the best breasts in the school. Even if the competition wasn't fierce, mine being a boys' school with few women teachers, nevertheless Miss Watkins' chest was a fine sight and she didn't mind who knew it. She taught French, she taught it with her handsome head up and her strong shoulders back, and she always had our full attention. Those were the days before girlie mags dominated the top shelf of every newsagent, and we were all fascinated by what it was—what they were—that filled and stretched Miss Watkins' blouse.

She knew this, and she tolerated it with a healthy good humour, until one day a boy named Smith, more daring than the rest, arranged for a friend to stumble against him when he (Smith) had gone up to ask Miss Watkins to explain one of the more irregular French verbs. Smith lurched into her bosom, and enjoyed it so much that he got his friend to repeat the stumble next day; and Miss Watkins, who disapproved of intellectual laziness, fetched Smith a clout with her copy of Progressive French Grammar that sent him spinning back to his desk like a dervish on bald tyres, and what's more she did it while keeping her finger in the book to mark her place, always the sign of a true professional.

Teachers thumped kids quite frequently in the Fifties. The notion of Pupils' Rights was unknown, and if it had been suggested it would have been ridiculed. The conflict was a two-way affair: there were certain masters whom you could 'play-up' and certain masters who clouted you. Occasionally the two came together in one man, and that was bad news all round. I remember a music teacher who always carried a chair-leg that still had bits of splintered wood sticking out. He boasted he had broken a boy's hand with it, and I believed him; but no matter how often he used it on us, he still couldn't teach us music. Then there was the PT master. He beat boys on the backside with a large wall-map of the world, rolled around the strip of wood from which it normally hung. He was short and stout, and the map was very long, so he had to stand well back in order to make his swing, a bit like W.C. Fields playing golf. When he got his follow-through right he could knock a boy clean off his feet.

Sex and authority: those were the dominant factors in the Fifties as I remember them. Sex was kept firmly in its place, which was out of sight, in the bedroom, between a married couple, not too often, preferably with the lights out. That didn't stop young people brooding about the subject but it ensured that precious little useful information reached them—officially, at any rate. At my school, the two periods of biology scheduled to cover human reproduction left many of us more confused than before. That tangle of plumbing created in chalk on the blackboard: did it really have something to do with our bodies? There was a rumour that sex was supposed to be fun. It didn't look like fun. The way the biology master described it, it sounded slightly less fun than unclogging a drain with a bent plunger.

On the other hand we were deep into adolescence and our genetic machinery was getting up a head of steam whether the rest of the world liked it or not, since the reproduction of the species had to proceed at any cost. As the Fifties began I was pretty sure that those bumps on the chest that made it so difficult for young ladies to bowl fast at cricket were probably a Good Thing, but how could I commit myself to a definite opinion when I hadn't so far actually seen them in the flesh? (Or seen it, since women didn't seem to know whether they had one bosom or two breasts. More confusion.) I couldn't put much faith in Smith's report of his collisions with Miss Watkins' frontage: Smith lied about everything, and in any case he was so short that he had to stand on his toes to get his nose in her cleavage. Nor could you learn a lot from kissing girls, except that God should have put the nose somewhere else, preferably behind the ears where it could continue breathing while the mouth was otherwise engaged. In the Fifties you couldn't tell anything from what was pressing against your Aertex shirt, because in those days breasts were made to fit bras, and not vice versa. What you felt during a steamy embrace were the sharp ends of two rugby balls, usually angled upwards like a pair of Bofors guns expecting enemy attack. Those bras were stoutly constructed and reinforced with piano wire, bits of Bakelite, and sterilised bottle-caps. If she suddenly got passionate they could give a chap a nasty bruise. Or two.

Indeed it wasn't until 1955 that I first saw a completely naked lady moving about. That was in a French film called *The Sheep Has Five Legs* (it was, of course, banned almost everywhere), and I realised that, unlike rugby balls, they swayed and trembled in a most attractive way. I was less enthusiastic about the discovery of pubic hair. This was wholly banned in the Fifties: never mentioned and certainly never shown in photographs or drawings of the female nude. After years of believing that all women were as smooth as marble from the neck down, like the Greek statues I had studied so closely, it took me a long time to adjust to this design-change, and even longer to approve of it.

Women were strange, distant creatures in those days, and I wasn't the only one to think so. Paul Hamlyn published *Every Girl's Handbook* slightly after the Fifties, in 1961. It included, under 'Etiquette', an item which sounds early-Victorian but was actually meant as useful advice to girls a generation ago:

'When passing an acquaintance in the street it is for the woman to

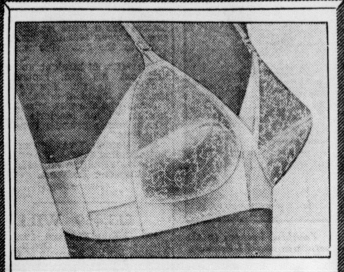

Playtex* Living* Bra

never slips, rides or slides !

Joy Mottram, famous tennis player, says "I find the Playtex Living Bra is absolutely perfect"

Jennifer Nicks, ice skating champion, says "It never slips or cuts however active I am. I always wear it."

The Rowe Twins, table-tennis stars, wear Playtex Bras for the wonderful freedom they give.

Try the bra that top sports figures wear

Here's the bra that top sports figures wear. The Playtex Living Bra. No matter how active you are it never slips, rides or slides.

Always — complete freedom and comfort. Such perfect shape and support, too. Sculptured nylon gently moulds you to the **lifted**, rounded American look.

Gleaming white elastic and nylon washes easily, needs no ironing, never loses its shape. Sizes 32 to 40. Cups A, B and C in most sizes.

27/6

* TRADE MARK © 1957

make the first sign of recognition, a man will not stop or raise his hat till he knows that she wishes to recognise him, nor will he stop to chat till she shows that she wishes to do so.'

Nobody ever told me that. But then, my grip of the gender game had taken a considerable beating at school, where the boys were under orders to address the mistresses as 'sir'. God knows how much damage this did to my already bewildered adolescent mind. There was a reason for it—the thinking was that, as school mistresses were a temporary aberration caused by the Second World War, a normal (all-male) service would obviously be restored as soon as possible, and by treating the ladies as honorary men it was possible to overlook the entire unfortunate business—but it was a pretty daft reason, especially as no school mistress wore slacks in those days. It was all part of a colossal conspiracy that infected the Fifties: a conspiracy to pretend that the war hadn't made any difference and that our reward for winning it was to go on living in the Thirties.

It was a popular conspiracy. After the Fighting Forties we were not yet ready for the Swinging Sixties. We wanted reassurance, orthodoxy, totally recognisable normality; we wanted to be quiet and comfortable again, so we slipped naturally back into the ways of living we had been accustomed to when our lives were so rudely interrupted by that ill-mannered thug, Hitler.

Not *all* the way back, of course. The politics of the Fifties were a long way from those of the Thirties, when (for instance) you might think twice before going to the doctor or dentist in case you couldn't afford his fee. Nothing was ever going to be the same after 1945. The troops came home, took one look at Churchill's policy for peace, and voted Labour in their millions. Or indeed after 1944, when the Education Act made it possible for working class boys like me to swim upstream to Oxbridge. But superficially the Fifties were an extension of the Thirties. The new cars looked pre-war because designers didn't know what post-war meant except it didn't mean 'austerity', the word that had come to summarise the bleak, rationed style of wartime goods. New clothes looked pre-war; there were fashion changes that moved hemlines but the significant thing is they usually moved them *down*, in celebration of the fact that we now had enough material to make really long skirts again. Nothing drastic happened to necklines, not down our street anyway. We hadn't fought two World Wars so that shameless hussies could go around exposing their chests and frightening the horses in the streets. (And you still occasionally saw horses in the streets in the Fifties, usually pulling milk floats or scrap-iron carts. Their dung did not long steam in the roadway. The nearest householder nipped out and scooped it up for his rhubarb. We had organic gardening before it was invented.) I can remember observing ladies' blouses that incorporated a kind of modesty veil to blur the plunge to cleavage. Hats were going out but those that were worn often had a bit of veil as a gesture to old-fashioned decency. Men's clothing was even more conventional. It boiled down to sports-jacket-and-flannels or single-breasted suit. You could get away with a sweater in the countryside. Desert boots? You wouldn't risk wearing them at the office; the boss might put you down as a poofter. I wore bottle-green corduroy trousers in 1955 and thought myself fairly daring. But it was the collar-and-tie that firmly shackled the

Fifties to the past.

There were three excuses for not wearing a tie: you were at the seaside, or you were in the bath, or you were dead; and I'm not sure the last was always good enough. In the Fifties, a collar and tie was like a label round your neck that told the world all it needed to know: how much money you had, what your politics were, where you'd been to school, and whether or not you slept in your vest.

No other country in the world had a tie industry that depended, not on taste and style, but on the accurate labelling of endless social divisions. The original purpose of the necktie was to keep the draught out of your shirt until buttons got invented, but in the Fifties men wore ties in order to give a clear advance warning of the sort of chap they were: Old Etonians or Tank Corps or MCC or Rutland University Chemistry Department Welsh Club Postgraduate Debating Society. The fact that most other people would not recognise the tie made no difference; quite the reverse. The whole point of a tie was to discourage outsiders: if you had to ask what it meant, then you didn't deserve to know. In the seventeenth century, Descartes said: I think, therefore I am. In the Fifties, British Man said: I know who I am because I've got the right tie on. (In the Eighties people said: I think I know who I am, because it says so here on my t-shirt.)

The tie itself was just the beginning. Much was revealed by the way you tied it. When I served in the RAF, for instance, the black uniform tie had to be knotted small and hard, halfway to strangulation: highly symbolic: the RAF wasn't interested in hearing what you had to say. The RAF gave you a separate collar which, when new, was as hard and shiny as sheet steel. It was anchored front and rear by studs that had to be rammed home like shipbuilders' rivets. Collars were, of course, starched; indeed the longer the decade went on the stiffer collars became until they were as tough as perspex. And the fashion was for increasingly cutaway collars; eventually the points went past twenty-to-four and reached nearly a quarter-to-three. I suppose we all thought we were expressing our personalities by wearing all that stuff; more likely we were expressing our lack of personality. But then, we hadn't clobbered the Hun so that men could be free to wear what they liked, had we? I mean, did we want the whole bloody country to go round looking like Teddy Boys? Not in the pub I used to drink in. The first time a Ted came in—inch-thick crepe soles, drainpipes, velvet collar, hair like Lassie— nobody spoke. All conversation stopped. He wasn't threatened or abused, he was simply frozen out. He swallowed his half of bitter and went.

Why did we despise him so much? The Teds were a working-class phenomenon but all classes resented their appearance. It was worse than facetious, it was ungrateful. *All those years of suffering and hardship, and this is how the rising generation thank us for it! Long stretch in uniform, that's what they need...* The fact that they *were* in uniform, but a uniform of their own choosing, got obscured by the fog of indignation. And the fact that it took a certain amount of courage to sport sideburns and a duck's-arse when the rest of the world was in short-back-and-sides was completely overlooked. The Fifties wanted stability and no big surprises. Teddy Boys threatened change, so they had to be wrong.

College Green: popular in the Fifties, as today, with office workers enjoying lunchtime sunshine.

I could never have been a Ted; I was far too obedient, too straight-arrow. When I was a teenager, the thing to do—the only thing there *was* to do—on a Sunday afternoon, was to meet your mates and Go for a Walk in the Woods: Blaise Castle Woods. The extraordinary thing is that for this scrambling, tripping, ball-hurling bit of mucking-about we all wore our best clothes. No jeans and trainers in those days; for us, sharply creased slacks and highly polished shoes. Completely inappropriate, but it must have satisfied a deep need. In the RAF I was quite proud of my uniform, and I pressed it so often that the tough fuzz of battledress was worn down to the smoothness of gabardine. At college, my freshmen's photograph shows a hundred-odd shiny young men, all in three-piece suits and tight, obedient smiles. (The last

15

time I was in Cambridge I saw the equivalent, modern-day picture in a photographer's window: it was all blue denim and cocky grins.)

No doubt the existence of National Service bolstered our respect for authority, our concern about appearance. National Service ended with the Fifties, and since then a sort of myth or legend has grown up, about what it was or did. There is a kind of Heavy Brigade who keep urging the return of conscription, not to repel the dreaded Russian juggernaut but to stop British youth from going to the dogs, and to try and get some of that damn hair off its head and onto its chest, not that you couldn't be sure they wouldn't all go home on leave and have it Marcelled, like the bunch of wishy-washy fairies they all are these days... Now, when I was in the army we had to do seven thousand push-ups every day before breakfast in full battle kit while the regimental band marched up and down on our backs playing 'Colonel Bogey'...

The truth about National Service is somewhat different.

First, the Services themselves didn't particularly want it. They reckoned, quite rightly, they could do a better job with volunteer professionals than they could with a lot of disgruntled conscripts.

Secondly, any benefit which British youth might have got would be despite—not because of—National Service, almost all of which consisted of standing around in heavy rain waiting for the transport to arrive.

In my two years in the RAF, I reckon I spent more soggy hours just standing with my hands in my pockets, gloomily watching the crease disappear from my battledress trousers, than Napoleon passed on Elba (also, as I recall, waiting for the transport to arrive).

It would have been nice to have been stationed on Elba. During squarebashing they asked us where we wanted to be posted. I wrote down Cyprus, Germany or Hong Kong, which the RAF interpreted to mean Exeter.

Every time I go through Devon, I look for something worth either (a) attacking or (b) defending, but Devon still looks to me like the least strategically important target in Britain with the possible exception of Rockall.

I suppose the naval dockyards at Plymouth might have been worth a bomb or two, but they were outside the range of the radar unit in which I earned my four bob (20p) a day. Later they gave us a great big shiny radar scanner with bucket seats and twin exhausts, which actually reached all the way to Plymouth, but it made no difference because none of our fighter squadrons could fly to Plymouth without running out of fuel on the way home.

Pretty well the only aircraft we tracked at all regularly was the milk flight from Guernsey to the mainland, which trudged across the Channel every morning at slightly more than Motorway speed. Occasionally something unidentified, sinister and spreading would appear on the screen, but it always turned out to be migrating ducks, although once it was the duty officer's tea, which had fallen into the gubbins.

Lacking anything much in the way of operations, the real work of the National Servicemen at RAF Exeter was to maintain the steady, even distribution of dust and dirt around the base. I passed many semi-conscious hours behind a broom. The idea was to harvest about six ounces of light rubbish, and then carefully steer it along the corridors and through the ops room. It was essential never to be seen standing still. On a quiet day, I might complete three or four laps of the radar block, shuffling at a disciplined half-a-knot, and finally handing over my six ounces of well-preserved litter to the next watch, from which another shuffler would be appointed to carry on guiding it around the linoleum circuit.

Those two years were not a complete waste of time, but this was no thanks to the authorities. My big benefit lay in learning how to play three-card brag. Gambling was illegal, so we hid the brag school from the eyes of the RAF police. One day the blanket fell off the window and a copper saw us. He hurried in, put the blanket back, and lost fifteen bob in thirty minutes. He hadn't had our practice, you see.

I also learned to cook light meals. This was necessary for survival while on fire picquet duty at night. Just before I got called up, a huge radar station in Suffolk had been gutted, so the RAF suddenly got very keen on having fire picquets. Considering the amount of unskilled cooking that went on throughout the night, it's a miracle the fire picquets themselves didn't burn down more radar stations. We were supposed to be fed by the main cookhouse, which was supposed to send us hot meals in large insulated containers. This was okay as long as you were crazy about tepid stew. What happened was the lads in the cookhouse simply chucked the day's dinner into the container and shut the lid. Thus what started out as roast pork with stuffing, peas and mash reached us, fifteen miles later, after a jolting journey over the Devon hills, as stew; and it was always tepid stew because, of course, the transport was always late.

So there you have it. Apart from three-card brag, light cooking, and stoic resignation in bus queues, I don't think I got anything valuable from my National Service. Some people might include the knowledge of how to whistle *The Skye Boat Song* while performing the slow march, I suppose, but not me. I could never understand why the drill instructors always chose that particular tune. Maybe it was to remind us that Bonnie Prince Charlie had his problems with sluggish transport, too.

Of course National Service didn't altogether stifle the spirit of young rebellion in the Fifties. Rock-and-roll took the youth of the country by storm; yet measured against the iron grip that Victor Sylvester and his ruthless, joyless strict tempo had imposed on the dance-floor, it was just a healthy shake-up, as the charleston and the black bottom had been a generation earlier. (None of it made any difference to me. I couldn't rock-and-roll any more than I could fox-trot. Some of us juss ain't born wid de riddum.) The *Lady Chatterley's Lover* case was a sensation, but in the Fifties you could create a sensation by saying 'Knickers!' on the wireless; indeed Muir and Norden, then scripting *Take It From Here*, had to get written permission from the BBC Head of Light Entertainment each time they wanted to use subversive language, such as 'nappies'. Even the title of D.H. Lawrence's book was not completely speakable. During the trial of the Penguin edition for obscenity, people wishing to buy an under-the-counter copy used to ask for 'The Lady'.

To realise just how authoritarian a country this was in the Fifties you have to remember not only that local Watch Committees had powers of censorship over films (long after the Fifties the Bristol committee banned a film at Arnolfini because they couldn't understand it and they thought audiences would be bored) but also that all stage plays were licensed by the Lord Chamberlain's office, whose officials could and did require cuts or changes. When Samuel Beckett wrote *End-Game* he included the line, 'I'd like to pee' and the word 'arses'—which, in 1958, to get the approval of the Lord Chamberlain, had to be changed to 'I'd like to relieve myself' and 'rumps'. A year earlier, John Osborne used 'ass-upwards' in *The Entertainer*; that had to be altered to 'cock-eyed'. One of the hit songs of the late Fifties was *Fings Ain't Wot They Used T'Be*, also the name of a hugely successful musical play. Included in the fings that weren't wot they used t'be were drink ('Once our beer was frothy, but now it's frothy coffee'—a dig at the new espresso bars), dance-halls ('They've changed our local palais into a bowling alley') and traffic ('There used to be trams, not very quick, but now there's just jams, half a mile thick'). But the great irony was this: the really important fings hadn't altered in the slightest, because the Lord Chamberlain felt obliged to devote much of his time to correcting the excesses of the musical *Fings*. Here are just a few of his instructions:

> The interior decorator is not to be played as a homosexual and his remark…"Excuse me, dear, red plush, that's camp that is," is to be omitted, as is the remark, "I've strained meself."

> The remark "Don't drink that stuff, it will rot your drawers" is to be omitted.

And my favourite:

> The builder's labourer is not to carry the plank of wood in the erotic place and at the erotic angle that he does, and the Lord Chamberlain wishes to be informed of the manner in which the plank is in future to be carried.

Why did we put up with such nonsense? I think we put up with it because we liked it, or at least we liked part of it. We liked the idea of order and regularity and control, the knowledge that—after the war years when, day in day out, you couldn't be sure that someone wouldn't try to kill you at any moment—it was reassuring to know that some aspects of life were utterly dependable; that you could take your maiden aunt to the theatre and be confident that you would get tea and biscuits served on a tray at your seats in the interval and you wouldn't be exposed to anything the Lord Chamberlain, bless his noble heart, suspected you might possibly find offensive.

All the more reassuring because the rest of the world—'bloody abroad' as Osbert Lancaster's Maisie Littlehampton used to call it—seemed to be going to hell. Overseas, the Fiftes were a pretty rackety decade, what with the Russians trying to blockade us out of Berlin; and the Korean War demonstrating that hordes of suicidal Chinese troops would, unless stopped, swim the Pacific and march ashore at Los Angeles which, as everyone knows, puts them within striking distance of Ilfracombe; and the Egyptians stealing (all right, nationalising) our Suez Canal (all right, so the Frogs built it) without which Britain could not survive (all right, so we survived for a couple of years without it) and forcing us very very reluctantly to invade them (all right, so it took us several months to get an invasion force organised) together with the Frogs and the Israelis who were equally determined to keep the Canal open (all right, so the Frogs hated the Wogs for supporting the Algerians who were fighting for independence and the Israelis wanted any excuse to get their own back against the Wogs) and it wasn't our fault the Egyptians promptly blocked the Canal (all right, so we should have expected that) and the Yanks told us to pull out fast or they'd hammer the pound until it looked like fourpence-ha'penny (all right, so we'd told Eisenhower a few little white lies, what did he expect when the Future of the Empire was at stake? (all right, so the Future of the Empire was Past) and the Prime Minister said President Nasser of Egypt was another Hitler (all right, so Eden had lost several of his marbles by then and Nasser resembled Hitler the way Russell Harty resembled Ivan the Terrible) and the whole sad, silly mess ended in tears. Meanwhile Russian tanks were charging into Budapest, Sputnik was circling the Earth, Britain was letting off umpteen H-bombs at Christmas Island while thousands of our brave troops (mostly National Servicemen) watched with complete and utter disregard for their own safety since they had no choice, the nearest land being five thousand miles away; and to make matters much, much worse there was an appalling Yank called Elvis Presley whose act looked like the kind of human-biology lesson I never got at school.

With the rest of the world so thoroughly unreliable, Britain in the Fifties adopted as its motto a song of the Thirties: *You Can't Do That There Here.*

And Bristol, as I remember it, was an enclave inside the island. With no InterCity or M4, London was remote: at least a couple of hours away by train and well over four hours by road, which was as it should be. If God had wanted Bristolians to commute to London, He would have called the city Reading, or even Slough.

Bristol was a fairly smug and self-centred place. You were born here, went to school here, got a job here—Wills, Frys or BAC—and died here. On the positive side, that way of life created a lot of useful social networks: for instance, the local 'Old Boy' rugby clubs—Old Elizabethans, Old Cothamians, Old Bristolians—got all their members from their respective schools. (Today they're open to anyone; the old boys have left town.) There were buses galore because few people had cars. Streets were clear and open. (When I was a kid I used to *rollerskate* along the Portway. Today, if I tried I'd probably get arrested, always assuming I didn't get killed first.) If you missed the last bus (and they usually packed up shortly before the pubs chucked out) you walked home. This never worried me. Was life safer then? It was certainly more law-abiding in some ways. When the lights on my bike failed, I didn't dare ride it in the dark because I knew I'd be stopped by a policeman. If I went to a soccer match my parents never worried about violence; there was none. Clubs and discos didn't yet exist, so you couldn't get into trouble there. If you wanted to go to the pictures you were spoiled for choice. If you didn't, you could go to the pub (and drink Real Ale before anyone called it that). Georges Brewery owned nearly all the pubs. Home-grown jazz—very trad stuff—was played in one or two. Eating out wasn't a problem because hardly anybody did it.

The truth is that Bristol in the Fifties was more than a bit self-satisfied and dull. Freighters still came up the Avon to unload in the City docks and there was an unspoken assumption that Bristol need never worry about its future because the world had always come to Bristol and always would. It was a good decade to be smug in. Harold Macmillan told us we'd never had it so good and he was right: you had to be very stupid not to get a job in the Fifties and totally illiterate not to find somewhere to live, because every newsagent's window was stuffed with cards advertising flats and bed-sits. When I went to work in London I just took the Tube to Maida Vale, scanned a few cards, rang a few doorbells and moved in. Dead simple.

I was a trainee copywriter in a biggish ad agency at £600 a year. I learned a lot about the Great British Public. I learned, for instance, that it had no navel; or if it had, it certainly didn't want to be reminded of the fact: most magazines and newspapers routinely required any ad that showed a naked stomach to have the navel airbrushed out. (Not surprisingly, ads for Tampax—one of our accounts—were banned by many women's magazines.) I learned that most people lie when they answer market-research question-naires: ask them how often they clean the loo, for instance. and they tell you what they think you'd like to hear. I once did a survey of grocers, asking them how much demand there was for a list of six products 'recently advertised on television'. The sixth product didn't exist; we'd invented it; but the grocers assured us the campaign was very effective. They didn't like to disappoint us. I learned Murphy's Law: If they *can* get it wrong, they *will* get it wrong. One of our accounts was Turf cigarettes. Everyone was offering free give-aways with fags. We had to join the crowd, so we offered Turf smokers something. We offered them a free pair of ex-Army socks. Some people sent them back, complaining that they wouldn't stay alight, or saying they preferred the cigarettes with spats on. I learned that the reason why the directors of Oldham Batteries were so willing to make so many arduous trips to London had less to do with approving new commercials than with being taken to see the strippers in Soho, presumably in order to reassure themselves about the survival of the navel.

I learned a lot in advertising but I never found out how to get my suit cleaned in less than three weeks. I took the suit to the Holborn High-Speed Rapid-Express Dry Cleaners, who promised it back in ten days. After ten days it wasn't ready and they told me to come back in a week, which I did, and it still wasn't ready, so I made disgruntled noises, and they got quite huffy. Did I realise, they asked, how far their van had to go to collect the dry cleaning? Hounslow! Had I seen the traffic between here and Hounslow? Murder, it was. Especially in this weather. What did I expect? Miracles?

There was something of the spirit of the Fifties in all that. It was not a dynamic decade. By the time I got my suit back the Fifties were nearly finished and in any case I had had enough of them. I went to America.

Alderman Hennessey's Bristol

Architect Michael Jenner looks back in anger
at the planning disasters

In 1938, not long after Munich, it was clear that we would almost certainly go to war with Germany. They had been preparing for it since Hitler came to power in 1933; we were totally unprepared. Over the next year there was a massive diversion of resources from peaceful to warlike purposes. When war was finally declared in September 1939 this diversion accelerated sharply and virtually all building stopped except for war purposes—munitions factories, military camps and canteens. When fighting began in earnest in 1940, building workers who had not been conscripted into the services were fully employed giving the minimum repair to buildings, roads and services after bombing, and on demolishing unsafe buildings. Many important buildings which could have been saved were demolished because there was no likelihood of repair for years to come. Building projects started before the war, such as Bristol's new Council House, were discontinued and boarded up.

At the end of the war there was not only the enormous accumulated task of rebuilding the bomb damage, there was also a shortage of most types of building, particularly housing, because nothing had been built for six years. There was scarcely any money to pay for it. The country's economic situation was worse than it had been for centuries, and was made worse still when the new Labour government embarked on an expensive series of social reforms probably greater than any in our history. So resources were literally rationed: some of them, such as bread, which had never been rationed during the war. Under those desperate circumstances building had to be rationed too, through a system of building licences, available only for essential works. So in our architectural history there is a gap of a decade, from mid 1938 to 1948, when scarcely anything which could be called architecture was built, and another few years after that when very little was built.

The national idealism and determination to change society—manifested in the landslide election of a Labour government—inevitably extended to architecture and planning. The mood was the precise opposite of today's. Where now conservation and restoration are almost a national obsession, then all was redevelopment and modernisation. Redevelopment plans took

little account of preserving old buildings, and new housing estates swept aside everything which existed on the site, from hedges and ponds to farmhouses and cottages. There were battles over whether a few obviously important buildings should be preserved, but there was widespread acceptance of the fact that great swathes of old cities should be destroyed in order to get the advantages of new development.

The great debate in architectural circles was the nature of modernism. I would guess that at least 90% of the profession in 1950 had accepted that modernism of some sort was inevitable and necessary. The question was which sort? At that time most architects considered that modernism was simply the latest style, a matter of using horizontal windows, white walls and flat roofs. To the minority of true believers that attitude was unforgivably frivolous. They refused to accept that modernism was a style, and therefore always referred to themselves as 'working in the Modern Movement'.

The Modern Movement was as much concerned with philosophy and ethics as it was with aesthetics. It was seen as the twentieth century's only logical and ethical way of designing buildings which took account of the economies which must inevitably follow the proper utilisation of the new technologies of steel, reinforced concrete and glass. Its protagonists believed passionately with the Austrian architect Adolf Loos that ornament was crime, since it diverted resources from more socially vital projects. Modern architects were frequently political in their dedication to mass housing, schools and hospitals.

All that idealism went sour in the 1960s. In the hands of a great genius such as Le Corbusier or Mies van der Rohe a largely ethical programme was sufficient, but in the hands of the earnest young architects who flocked in the 50s to local authority and hospital architects' departments, it was quite inadequate. I can make no attempt here to defend the building which appeared in the 1960s, but two things are incontrovertible. The first is that the pendulum of taste is now at its furthest point from the architecture of that time, making it impossible to distinguish the good from the bad. The second is that the best of the architects who designed and the councillors who commissioned were intensely idealistic. The high-rise flats, to take one example, were not the product of a cynical disregard for people's happiness, as is so easily assumed today. In other countries people had lived in flats for decades or even centuries, and were perfectly happy. There seemed no reason to suppose that Britons would be any different. The designers believed they would improve people's lives, not spoil them. The reasons why it all went wrong are outside the time scope of this book, but the idealism and sense of purpose which went into it grew up in the 50s.

I am tempted to describe the work during the 50s of the few True Believers in Bristol. But I am forced to admit that when added together it amounts to very little. What's more, I don't now consider that what then seemed to be an impassable gulf between us and them really amounted to anything significant. 'We' consisted principally of Towning Hill and Partners; Tom

College Street houses before demolition for municipal car parking. It is almost inconceivable that these Georgian gems would be swept away today.

Burrough; the architect's department of E.S. & A. Robinson under John Collins (which I joined for 4 years in 1954); and for a very few years up to about 1951 when the brilliant assistant architect David du R. Aberdeen left them, the architects' department of BAC. The other camp consisted of a few architects I now deeply respect, such as Eustace Button and Ralph Edwards, others such as the City Architect's Department, whose work was seldom outstanding but always decent, and one or two big commercial practices whose work at that time I still regard with contempt.

In 1950 the key architectural event in Bristol was the imminent completion of the Council House. The architect was Vincent Harris, who had specialised in town and county halls. At his best he was a decent second-rate architect, but Bristol is his worst town hall by a considerable margin. Here and at the Taunton County Hall he was under the influence of Sir Edwin Lutyens, as almost every architect in Britain was bound to be at some time between the 1890s and the 1930s. Some of the smaller details on the Council House, such as the stone bollards around College Green, are stolen from Lutyens complete, which has always seemed fairly outrageous to me. But every Bristol architect, whichever camp he was in, considered him totally outrageous because, in effect he had stolen the commission. He was first appointed by the City Council to judge a competition for the building. The story of how he managed to have the competition, and his fellow assessor the President of the Bristol Society of Architects, set aside and himself appointed, has been told by Bryan Little in *Bristol: the Public View* (Redcliffe Press).

The worst feature of the building is the huge, harsh roof. It is absurdly steep and high, like that of a French palace, but without the elaborate dormers, pavilions and twiddly bits which make French roofs such fun. It's true that he wanted to furnish it with an expensive decorative cresting which the Council jibbed at, but that was simply a problem he had to solve, if necessary by reducing the height of the roof. I can't see Time ever making the roof acceptable, or the boring rows of identical windows either. But though the whole is gross, some of the parts are enjoyable. My favourite bit is the row of gigantic columns along the pavement of Frog Lane just before it goes under Park Street, and the great stair that goes down to it. That's real urban architecture, and I suspect that for once Harris was being himself and not cribbing Lutyens.

Harris was clearly given a very large budget. The building materials, from the beautiful handmade bricks, which are longer and thinner than standard, to the marble of the entrance hall and the panelling of the committee rooms, are magnificent, and Cowlin's superb craftsmanship is beyond praise. Few of Bristol's genuine Georgian buildings are as well built as this fake one.

The building has other pleasures for the observant, such as the only two windows singled out for special treatment. They are at first floor level inside the high arched pavilions at each end of the curved facade facing onto College Green. Each window, with its framing columns and balcony front, will have cost as much as a couple of council houses. They are more magnificent, though much smaller, than the balcony at Buckingham Palace on which kings and queens appear on state occasions. To be Lord Mayor of

Hartcliffe: 'Almost every big mistake which can be made in the design of a housing estate'.

Bristol and have a window like that in your parlour would be glory indeed. But when you peer in the windows you don't see the Lord Mayor, or the Town Clerk or even the City Architect, you see a row of Twyford's patent WC cisterns. All that splendour for a couple of loo windows! In the 1950s that detail summed up the absurdity of that sort of grandiose fancy dress building. It wasn't merely absurd, it was criminally absurd,for exactly the reasons which Adolf Loos had said. Hidden inside their pavilions they contribute very little to the overall design of the Council House. What's more, Vincent Harris must have known that. He would not have done it if he thought people would ever look up at the windows. He was a cynic without any design principles at all.

At that time in Bristol very few people outside the profession were much interested in architecture, or could be bothered with the philosophy of the Modern Movement. One man who did was Crofton Gane, the Quaker owner of a well known furniture shop in Park Street. When Marcel Breuer fled to Britain from Nazi Germany in 1936, Gane kept him alive for a while by giving him a commission for a show house in an exhibition on the Downs. It only lasted a few months but it has passed into history. It was influenced by Mies van der Rohe's famous Barcelona show house of 1929, but built on a much smaller budget. It was the first time that Mies's play of floating roof planes hovering over walls conceived as planes (without being pierced for doors or windows) was seen in Britain in such diagramatic clarity, but it introduced something new of its own into architecture. Until then Modern Movement walls were invariably white concrete or stone, or just occasionally a puritanical pale brick. Possibly because of the tiny budget, Breuer made his walls of rubble stone. This great enrichment of the vocabulary, both in colour and texture, proved enormously influential when Breuer moved on to the United States, and from there after the war it returned to influence British architecture, particularly the schools of the 50s and 60s. Gane also commissioned Breuer to design the furnishings and interior of his house in Downs Park, which are now in the Museum. I got to know him shortly after I started my own practice in 1958, and I remember my surprise at finding that extraordinary interior in that ordinary house.

One man who didn't know anything about architecture or the modern movement was Alderman Hennessey, said to be the virtual dictator of architectural and planning matters in the city. I remember seeing him once, when he arrived at a public lecture surrounded by a retinue of senior city architects and planners. He looked like a retired nightclub bouncer and could scarcely wait to get up and tell us how he was going to rebuild this useless city built by exploiters of the poor during the Industrial Revolution. It took me a minute or two to realise that the term Industrial Revolution, which he used constantly, meant the entire nineteenth century and any bits of other centuries which happened to include events of which he disapproved but didn't know the date. His combination of ignorance and self-satisfaction was breathtaking. I have learnt since that he was a genuine hero of the labour movement in Bristol between the wars, but in the 1950s he and his type, with their hatred of the past equalled only by their ignorance, their contempt for learning and reflection, and their determination to transform Bristol without knowing what they were doing, or giving anybody a chance to consider how it ought to be, were to cause untold damage.

The worst instance was the building of Hartcliffe. I have mentioned the huge housing problem, caused not so much by the bombing as by the fact that since 1939 there had been no new building. As a result there was a decade of new families to catch up with. Everywhere in Britain, the 1950s saw the planning of huge new estates whose designers had learnt nothing from the lessons of the pre-war estates. Almost every big mistake which can be made in the design of a housing estate was made at Hartcliffe, and most of them had been made at Knowle West or elsewhere before the war.

In the first place, Hartcliffe is much too big. It has roughly the same population as Bridgwater, about 26,000 people, but with only a minute proportion of its facilities: 3 or 4 pubs instead of dozens, a few dozen shops instead of hundreds. Everybody who moved in was married with one or two children (or they didn't have enough points to qualify), so all the adults and children were in roughly the same age brackets. When the now familiar problems of housewives' estate-induced loneliness and boredom appeared, there were soon hundreds of cases. The children, all growing up together, were packed into a single secondary school, which was the largest comprehensive in Bristol, a city of over-big comprehensives. When they reached the difficult years, they reached them together.

What was almost as bad, though less mentionable nowadays, is that these

The doomed Brandon Flats in Jacobs Wells Road shortly before demolition in 1957.

giant estates were all one class. There were not only no grannies, with their remarkable calming and civilising effect, there were scarcely any middle class people either: few people accustomed to giving a lead, who knew how to complain effectively, or how to get things done. In 1960, when the population was already 16,000 (the size of Chippenham), there were just six professionally qualified people living at Hartcliffe. I don't suppose the proportion is very different now, for who would choose to live there. It's miles from anywhere, and on no through routes. The few shops have a captive market, which usually means that prices are high and service poor. In the early days Hartcliffe people compared the dismal quality of their local shops with the eagerly competing service in the shops where they had grown up. As I have already said, when the 1950s estates were built, all existing features were bulldozed. To this day they are bleak and unlovely places. The design was worthy but dull and boring. They look what they were, places thrown up in a hurry.

Whenever their shortcomings are mentioned, the same excuse is always made—that the housing problem at the time was so acute that there was no alternative, no opportunity for thought or research. I've no doubt that's how it seemed at the time, but it's a grossly inadequate excuse to say that you spoilt thousands of people's lives, at least to some extent, in order to help a few of them in the short term by starting a little earlier.

One has to say in fairness that many other big cities in Britain made the same mistakes. Abroad, some countries did better, some worse. It's easy to criticise in retrospect, but necessary if we are to avoid repeating our mistakes. The same applies to Bristol's other great planning disaster of the 1950s, Broadmead. It's an awesome thought that Bristol possibly built the most inept major shopping centre in the world.

In the 1930s Bristol's main popular shopping area was centred on Castle and Wine Streets, both consisting mostly of eighteenth century houses converted to shops. There are many published descriptions of what the area was like, crowded with people on Saturday nights. It was almost entirely destroyed by the blitz of 1940 and 1941. Rebuilding was essential and the City Council decided to rebuild on a different site, in the area around Broadmead. I suppose a new site was logical because it meant that the few shops which had not been destroyed could remain in use until the new ones were ready. But it had several evil effects which were probably not apparent at the time.

The study of cities and how they work is not yet an exact science; in 1940 it had scarcely begun. Such ignorance had seldom mattered previously because the changes which occurred in most cities were relatively minor and happened piecemeal. On the few occasions when major surgery had taken place, as in Paris in the 1860s, it was probably as much luck as judgement that it worked so well. In any case Continental traditions of absolutism made major changes more common there than in Britain, where the historic concern for liberty and freedom meant that public authorities had much more difficulty in carrying them out. The improvements which Joe Chamberlain initiated in Birmingham, for example, took a long time to achieve, and were bitterly contested. But their huge success, in both social and economic terms, were an enormous encouragement for other cities to follow suit. The novel idea of borrowing money to pay for slum clearance, and paying back the loans from the huge rate income which the subsequent redevelopment produced, was very seductive. Unfortunately few local politicians have ever had Chamberlain's abilities.

What Bristol City Council in the 1940s had not noticed was that the pre-war Castle Street/Wine Street shopping area was part of a continuous line of shops which stretched right across the city. It began at Blackboy Hill, went down Whiteladies Road, through Queens Road and Park Street, and achieved its social climax with the poshest shops on College Green. It then went up Clare and Corn Streets and reached its popular climax in Wine and Castle Steets, and the complex of other streets around them. It continued up Old Market, then still enormously popular but slipping down the social scale, and out along Stapleton Road to the eastern part of the city. The decision to rebuild in the Broadmead area broke that continuous line. No one can say

Acres of buildings like these were destroyed by the planners for the new Broadmead shopping area.

for certain that the deterioration which subseqently occurred in the two truncated ends of the line was due to the surgery, but it does seem very likely. There was an almost immediate effect in Old Market and Stapleton Road—both of which must have lived to some extent off their connexion to Castle Street—and there has been a slower deterioration in Park Street. The disappearance of shops from College Green was due to the bombing, but their loss had a marked effect on the fortunes of the shops at the bottom of Park Street and round the corner in the Centre.

Possibly someone at the time was conscious of the continuous line having been broken, because a tenuous shopping link between Broadmead and Old Market was constructed, with a row of new shops in Lower Castle Street. They were never a success and were demolished in 1970.

The second evil effect of the decision to relocate is incontrovertible: it destroyed the fascinating Broadmead district. I must try to put aside hindsight and be as accurate as I can in remembering how I felt about that. I first got to know something of Bristol at the end of 1945 and early 1946 when I lived here for several months. I was 17 and didn't take an intelligent interest in the city, but I saw enough to realise what a delightful place it was. When a few years later I came out of the army I chose the Bristol School of Architecture quite as much for the city as for the reputation of the School. I became a student in 1949 and immediately set out to know the city. I remember the Broadmead area fairly well. It was run down, but then everywhere in Europe was run down after the bombs and ten years without maintenance. I suppose it must also have been suffering from what we later learnt to call planning blight. It was a district very little altered since 1900, a delightful tatty mix of mostly Georgian and early Victorian buildings. There were still lanes and alleys of cottages opening off the streets, and secret over-grown gardens and burial grounds which I stumbled on by chance. I know now, though I didn't then, that most English towns had rather similar areas, and there were other parts of Bristol where one could still explore forgotten lanes and courts and come upon marvellous old buildings mouldering away in genteel or occasionally depraved poverty. I don't believe that a single district of that sort can now remain in Britain, though plenty survive on the Continent. We swept all ours away in a tragic outburst of nannyish tidying up and improvement.

If the old Broadmead existed today it would be recognised as a unique national treasure, but even now we would be unable to resist tidying it up, renewing the patched and peeling render, and putting the smelly old inhabitants into bright new flats with wardens. I remember the little shops where men in stiff shiny suits and shirts without collars would mend chairs, or sharpen saws, or gild picture frames. I remember the magnificent Victorian Penn Street Tabernacle towering over the little houses. But, and this is the point, I also remember very clearly that it never occurred to me to question the wisdom of pulling it all down. In that respect I was typical of the overwhelming bulk of the population. There were people who objected, but they were a tiny minority. About two years later I began to get to know some of them and they opened my eyes. In any case I could soon see for myself that it wasn't only Broadmead which was being demolished, it seemed to be every old district in the city. And finally, of course, I began to see what was going up in Broadmead to replace the old buildings.

Years later in 1972, as one of the most frustrating jobs I ever had, I was commissioned by the Council to advise on the pedestrianisation of Broadmead. I spent some time going through the planning archives to see how a perfectly competent city architect and city planning officer could have

After Hitler came the planners and the road builders. The remains of St James'
Square were soon to disappear under the bulldozer.

made such a mess. The truth is that their first ideas, drawn up in 1944 before
the end of the war, were praiseworthy. At that time you had to be a visionary
to conceive that the growth of motor vehicles would soon make traffic and
pedestrian segregation necessary. In contemporary Coventry and Rotterdam
visionaries did that; in Bristol the Alderman Hennessey type weren't going to
have any nonsense of that sort. The architectural style proposed in the 1944
plan was the sort of stripped classicism that Sir Basil Spence frequently used
20 years later. It would now be thought a little dry but would be treated with
respect. The layout was the splendid old Beaux Arts pattern that

Abercrombie used at Plymouth at the same time, with streets arranged on formal axes. I think it was too formal for shopping streets, but it would have been an excellent example of its type. As drawn, I think it was better than Plymouth as built.

But compromise followed compromise, and architectural unity and the grand layout were shattered. As it was built it isn't a patch on Plymouth, and Coventry is in a different class altogether.

I have no doubt that formality was the cause of the wreck. There are two ways of designing a street, either as a classical unity, where the parts give up their individuality to the whole, or as a picturesque assemblage, where the whole is made up of a variety of disparate, even antagonistic, bits. The latter, despite Bath, is the English tradition, exemplified in ten thousand High Streets throughout the country.

In Broadmead the gentle, gentlemanly City Architect fought to preserve his classical unity against the sharks of commerce, aided and abetted by the City Valuer and a council quite properly more concerned with finance than formality. Art and the City Architect never had a chance. The result was the worst of all worlds. The council couldn't impose a unified design on the retail chains, but they did insist on a unified height and on Bath stone. The result is a bore because there is no real variety and no grand unifying vision. Very few architects could have done much better with that particular set of criteria. In my opinion the only way anybody then—or now—could achieve success would be to swim with the current. I don't think it wrong for traders to behave like hucksters and want to out-shout their competitors with bolder or brassier buildings: they have always done so and have produced splendidly vigorous streets in the process. 999 out of every 1,000 shopping streets have gone for variety, not unity. To be successful they need as little control as possible. Vulgarity very rarely hurt a shopping street; boring good taste kills them. Few planners, whose jobs depend on society accepting that control is better than anarchy, and gentility better than vulgarity, will ever accept that.

The original 1944 design preserved only one or two of the more notable existing buildings on the site, contentedly condemning hundreds of others, including the arcade. The design which was actually built preserved five. Nobody who did not know the city in those years can understand why I, and the overwhelming majority of Bristolians, were content to accept that destruction, or most of it. I think almost everybody believed that the new buildings would be an improvement on the old ones; cleaner, more logical, more useful and more comfortable. In any case Bristol had so many old buildings, thousands and thousands of them, it could easily afford to lose a few hundred here and there. It was only when the destruction went on and on, and we began to realise that the whole character of the city was changing, that the movement to stop the destruction really began in earnest.

Even in the 40s, of course, there were battles to save particular buildings. The arcade is a case in point. The Upper Arcade had been destroyed by bombs, but the Lower half, of 1824, survived, occupied mostly by seedy traders. I'm quite sure that the reason it was scheduled for demolition was because it didn't fit into the grand 1944 plan, but the reason given publicly was that there was no other way of getting rid of the rats (how many times was I to hear that in the coming years!). There was a row and it was the City Architect himself who intervened to save it. All honour to him, but he then gave way to the interests of the new traders and substantially spoilt it, which included destroying the last surviving Regency shop front with its knife-thin copper glazing bars.

The Broadmead layout as finally built was simply the old pattern of corridor streets with service courts behind. I remember a lecture which the chief, or perhaps the deputy, planning officer gave when I was a student. He clearly despaired of Broadmead but he spent ten enthusiastic minutes telling us how he fought Woolworths to stop them having their usual brash red fascia, and how he finally won and they put up something more tasteful. I thought he was a fool: he had worn himself out by fighting the wrong battles. He should have let the traders have much more freedom—almost total freedom on their facades—and he should have sorted out Quakers' Friars. I have written on that subject so often that I don't want to go into it again at any length, but the old buildings in Quakers' Friars are a tiny delightful island surrounded by parking and the blind ugly backs of the shops around. When wedding parties come out of the Register Office the first sight they see is a row of dustbins and paper sacks. If the shops had been turned back to front, which, very roughly speaking is what they did with the whole shopping centre in Coventry, then the refuse carts and delivery lorries could have used the streets, and the shoppers could have used the space around Quakers' Friars. In 1972 I suggested how something of that could still be done by building another row of shops between the old buildings and the 1950s shops, which would make a surprisingly large new pedestrian square. In the middle the old Quakers' Friars buildings would at last look at home. My suggestions got no further than those of the City Architect and the Planning Officer 20 years before. None of my ideas were carried out then, though a few minor ones, such as the brick paving, have been done subsequently. I expect eventually most of the others will too.

So what went wrong, what lay behind the failure of the 1950s and caused many of the horrors of the 60s and 70s? I'm afraid my answer treads heavily on political toes. I can only say that I didn't arrive at it politically, it grew out of a lifetime of professional practice. And it isn't a conclusion I came to recently. I first put it into print in 1969. The reason was too much intervention and control by authority.

Just consider the disasters which have afflicted council houses and flats. They were built by idealistic councillors inspired by a generous dream, yet the estates are unpopular, windswept and bleak. The flats are unpopular, often vandalised, and the common parts are unkempt. Houses and flats are frequently falling apart, so much so that the national bill for putting right their technical defects is astronomical. It's impossible to look at British post-war council housing objectively and deny that on the whole it has been a failure.

Then consider the larger number of private houses and flats. They were built (like eighteenth century Bath) by speculators for profit. They are often tasteless and sometimes appallingly so, which is hardly ever the case with council housing. Contrary to popular belief they are often smaller than

Rosemary Street being re-made and widened to serve the Broadmead shops.

equivalent council housing, and were usually built more cheaply. But they are popular, always beautifully maintained and never vandalised. They were all as bleak as the council estates when they were new, but within five years they were beautifully set in trees and shrubs. They scarcely ever suffer from technical defects. All the traps into which the councils fell—such as system building or high rise—were avoided by the spec builders because they were too expensive and too wasteful of land. The councils honestly thought they knew what was best for their tenants; the spec builders did know what their customers wanted. Those that didn't know, went out of business.

Broadmead failed because the council misguidedly tried to control the traders. Some control is needed, but Broadmead has had far too much. Really effective city planning began in 1946. Is it coincidence that it's *precisely* the 40 years since then which have witnessed greater urban devastation than any other period in our history? It's impossible to look at British post-war cities objectively and deny that on the whole town planning has been a failure.

Of course we need some council housing, but not much. Of course we need town planning, but much less than we get. In planning, the crucial job for the 1990s is to sort out just what we do need and to drop what we don't.

Salad Days

Helen Reid recalls university life in the Fifties

Things I took with me when I came up to Bristol as a student in 1954: a ration book (food rationing was in its last gasp); a harlequin teaset (all the rage after the Festival of Britain); my bicycle (I did not realise Bristol had hills) and a big trunk full of grown-up clothes.

I came on the steam train from Paddington, a two and a half hours journey and found Richmond Hill. After suburban London, the hills were astonishing; I spent my first three weeks with aching legs, and a desire to sleep round the clock: Bristol air made you extraordinarily somnolent.

Bristol in 1954 still showed raw scars from the blitz: Park Street was full of gaps, like missing teeth, bombsites where Herb Robert grew. There was still a British Restaurant on College Green; Gillows on the Triangle had not yet been built, and the Broadmead development (we only went there to visit Marks and Spencer and buy boys' shirts) had only begun piecemeal.

But the cinemas were still going strong; The Embassy, in Queens Avenue, the Academy in Cheltenham Road, the Tatler in Old Market, all prized because they showed Continental films. Bristol Old Vic was entering its O'Toole era of greatness and the Colston Hall had many more classical concerts than it has now.

But for students, Bristol meant Clifton, Redland, a bit of Cotham and The Centre: when I left the University and started work, I was amazed to find how huge the city was, and how ugly parts of it were.

Our lives centred round the halls of residence, the Union, then at the Victoria Rooms, and the University buildings: we plodded these routes every day, on foot and bike (only a tiny percentage of students had cars).

In between lectures, the Arts students made like homing pigeons for The Berkeley: upstairs if you were posh and liked to listen to the trio, but usually downstairs at the back, under the dome, where for the price of a cup of coffee, 6d, you could argue, gossip and above all, eavesdrop: the dome had the peculiar acoustic effect of amplifying private conversations being carried on yards away.

On Saturdays, like middle-aged people, we went to the cafe in Brights, and had waitress service, or had an ice-cream soda in Forte's, opposite, sitting in Lloyd Loom chairs.

In fact though we didn't know it, we were elderly before our time. There was no youth cult in the early Fifties: you left school and became an adult overnight. So in our student luggage, there were no blue jeans, no teeshirts, no packets of contraceptive pills; we had no youth music of our own other than skiffle and bop, no fashions of our own. Women's Lib had not been invented, there were no drugs, and I can't remember ever seeing a television set in my student years.

Social life hinged on hops: there were about ten dances and balls a term. Mostly they were cattle markets held at the Vic Rooms, where the 'men' gathered in groups round the bar (orange juice in half pint beer mugs, 3d a glass, was popular) while the girls hugged the walls, waiting to be singled out and kicked to pieces in the quickstep, under the flicking lights of the witchball.

Like Cinderella, every girl wanted to go to THE Ball, in this case the annual Union Ball, a most formal affair where officers of other unions were invited, and the top men were expected to wear tails.

When the great day came, your partner, if he was properly trained, would present you with a corsage and hand you into a taxi, with your stole and your evening bag, your long gloves and your agonising high heels, for a night of stunningly middle-aged entertainment.

We all sat down to an austere institutional dinner, the Sauternes flowed like Tizer, and there were heavily witty undergraduate speeches, loyal toasts and singing of the University song, pinched from Gilbert and Sullivan.

'Though I myself have said it, and it's greatly to my credit, I am a Bristol man,' sang the girls. Sexism was as yet undiscovered. 'For I might have gone to Manchester, or Liverpool or Exeter, or even Birmingham (hold nose and pull imaginary chain). But in spite of all these colleges, which are really just apologies, I remain a Bristol man'.

Then we'd dance the night away under the witchbowl in the Victoria Rooms, and stagger home feeling terribly worldly and stylish.

In the Fifties, Bristol University was hop-mad: There were freshers hops, bophops, OpSoc hops, DramSoc hops, and even, after exams in the summer, tea-dances, held every day of the week in the Berkeley. It was the legitimate way to meet members of the opposite sex: you announced your credentials, what you were reading, what year you were in, whether you lived in hall or digs, and you clicked, or you didn't. If you did, you went to yet another hop, or to the pictures, or to tea in hall.

Hall, in my case Manor Hall, was an extension of boarding school, an impression which was reinforced when I learned the Head of Hall was a girl named Charity Vanstone: pure Angela Brazil. Hall was single sex of course, and hemmed in by rules. You could stay out until 10pm, or apply for a late pass until 11pm, and in the evenings, if you went out, you had to sign a book on leaving, saying where you were going, and again on returning.

Men were allowed to visit, if they signed in, and then you could offer them coffee in your room, made on a gas-ring, or you could take them to the Common Room. It was understood that we were on our honour to Behave, as it was delicately put and most of us did in that pre-Pill age, from fear rather than morality.

36

*The student rag was a
big occasion back
in the Fifties.*

*Photographs courtesy:
City of Bristol University*

On Saturday nights, when it was a mark of inferiority not to be going out, the Warden would cry as we left in our bophop finery: 'Don't hang around with the chaps!'.

This of course was what we intended to do. At curfew time, couples would congregate in the kindly shadows outside Hall, saying goodnight, and on the stroke of 11pm, the lights in the grounds would snap on, and we would all spring apart with nervous laughter, caught hanging around with the chaps. . .

Hall provided everything: three meals a day, optional prayers in the morning, a library, a 'quiet room' where evangelical girls would keenly invite you to come and meet Jesus, laundry rooms, kitchens, and above all friendship. At dinner, which was formal, we wore our gowns, and there was a High Table, where staff sat: if you were late, you had to stand below High Table, wait until you caught an academic eye, bob, and then go to your place.

Academically in the Fifties, Bristol University had a good reputation, especially for English, Engineering, Medicine, Physics and Education; even then competition to get in was fierce and Bristol had a social cachet as well as being the refuge for public school pupils who could not make it to Oxford or Cambridge.

We would not have dreamed of questioning the syllabus we had to follow, or of expecting any kind of democracy in the running of the university; student sit-ins and representations on committees were years ahead. We wore our gowns at all times, were known as Miss or Mister, and had very little social contact at all with academic staff. For we were a docile crew, fruits of the Butler Education Act, and mindful of the privileges we were enjoying. We knew we were a privileged three per cent of the population, having a three year holiday from responsibility: we were after all the new children of the Welfare State, and on the whole we worked hard—there were few drop-outs, in an age when drinking, smoking, and conspicuous consumption were not the fashion, and drugs had not arrived.

One day at the beginning of term, when we all surged over to the Berkeley after a ten o'clock lecture, a middle-aged man coming out was mown down in the crush. A waitress helped him up. 'What in God's name was that?' he asked indignantly. 'Oh, it's Them, They're back.' said the waitress, with deep resignation, and I realised with a tinge of guilt that people like them were paying taxes so we could be educated.

But we could not have been picked out as students in a crowd: men wore blazers and flannels, or cords if they were arty, girls wore long full skirts with paper taffeta petticoats, jersey tops and ballerina shoes, and in the winter, tweed suits. The only fashion fad was for the girls to wear tight black drainpipe trousers and cardigans worn back to front, or men's sweaters. We were only identifiable from our contemporaries by the fact that we wore gowns in the street, and faculty scarves.

In any case we had very little money, for grants were: miniscule: I had £175 a year as an undergraduate, after hall and tuition fees were paid, and £250 a year as a postgraduate, and this paid for clothes, books, travel, and later food and rent, which was 30s a week for an alarmingly dank and gloomy basement flat with a bath in the kitchen.

Royal York Crescent before gentrification. In the Fifties the streets were without cars but the houses were full of student flats and bedsits.

In an age when there were few paperbacks, book bills were enormous. Georges Bookshop, then just the one building on the corner of Berkeley Square, was the cause of my first-ever overdraft, £80 which took a year of my first earnings to pay off.

So of course we had to have 'vac jobs.' Mine ranged from tomato-picking and soap-packing, to working in Clifton Woolworths, where pay and morale were so abysmal that we used to sit under the counters on the floor and ignore the customers, and have enlightening gynaecological chats. I also worked in Jones's, newly opened in 1957, as a waitress, learning the mysteries of silver service, and in Lewis's, before it opened, and then later in the hated Haberdashery and Hardware.

It was thanks to Lewis's, in a way, that I ended up as a journalist. For several vacations, I worked in their publicity department, along with a young lay-out artist who wrote plays and was called Charles Wood, and this experience was counted when I applied for a job on the *Bristol Evening Post*. In the extraordinary job-rich world of the Fifties, the Labour Exchange in Nelson Street sent me along for this interview, for a job it had never occurred to me to try for.

For we were privileged; in the Fifties, with a degree, you could walk into work anywhere, and many of us chose our subject without any view to a career. I was unusual in that I didn't want to teach, unlike everyone else in my year; after going to the University Appointments Board, where I was told 'there was good work to be done in Africa,' I declined that option politely and went on the dole for six weeks, until I happened on what turned out to be a lifetime's career, just by chance. Jobs then just grew on trees.

This is not to say that we were not serious-minded: we were the war baby generation and we didn't expect much; we were unmaterialistic, unacquisitive, and on the whole unquestioning of authority. The male students still had to do National Service; University mock elections returned a Conservative with unfailing regularity; Union debates toed the establishment line.

We were apolitical on the whole, though there was a Communist Party student branch; it had ten members. And then into this safe world came Suez.

For the first time in years, students found a voice, and there were daily packed debates, in which opinion divided down the middle: the anti-Eden faction only won by a narrow majority.

It was the first time for years that Bristol students had become really involved in politics, enough to hold a protest march (the word demo hadn't arrived) and this awakening was further heightened by events in Hungary soon after. But neither event had a long-lasting politicising effect as far as I could see.

In any case, what students got up to in the Fifties, apart from Rag, rarely ever aroused the interest of real Bristol. Rag Week was mostly an excuse for junketing, and the actual object of raising money for charity did not seem to loom large in our minds. Our chief aim was to dress up exotically—I remember for some obscure reason being kitted out as a bee one year—and ride on a brewer's dray. The rest of Bristol, as ever, was tolerant of our

The other George's Bookshop: Mr George was a common sight standing outside his secondhand bookstore on Christmas Steps.

excesses, which in fact were very mild.

For as now, there was not much mingling of Town and Gown. We thought we owned crumbling and slightly Bohemian Clifton, and left the rest of Bristol to get on with it. I don't remember being aware what the politics of the Corporation were, or what local issues were: students never read the local papers.

The issues of the day were housing, the rebuilding of the city, and in particular Broadmead, the future of Castle Park area, then a mournful desert of rain-filled craters, car parks and the solitary Co-op store, with its Mantles Department. The only socially responsible project undertaken by students was to help at the Docks Settlement in Barton Hill. And yet the city impinged, got into our bloodstream. Lunchtimes spent on Brandon Hill, eating granary bread and cheese purchased at Cater Stoffel and Fort, in Queens Road, drinking at The Quinton and Aunties, visits to the City Museum, sorties into Bristol's first Chinese restaurant, The Chop Stick in the Triangle (three courses, 2s. 11d.) and the first espresso bar underneath Berkeley Place, in a basement where you could drink a glass cup of coffee-flavoured froth for 9d, walks on the Downs and in Leigh Woods, parties in dilapidated flats in Clifton: you missed all this when you went back home.

So much so that hundreds and hundreds of students lingered on in Bristol, many for life. Acclimatised to the hills, we stopped coming up and going down each term, as the student jargon had it, and stayed put.

The Beautiful Brab

A failure . . . or a success? asks James Belsey

Poor, shabby post-war Britain...it so desperately needed symbols to cling to and no symbol came quite as big and as bold as the Bristol Brabazon.

The war had been won but you wouldn't know it during the drab years of austerity immediately after VE and VJ days. Britain was a cold, lack-lustre, comfortless place, its cities scarred by bombing, its buildings dowdy for lack of paint, its citizens poorly dressed and food meagre as rationing went on and on and on.

Schoolchildren like me could actually watch Britain going downhill. The world map kept changing as the reassuring Imperial pink which had spread a flush across pre-war atlasses gave way to a new, unfamiliar jigsaw of multicoloured countries. Britain's place as one of the world's great powers was slipping through our fingers and everyone knew it. To make matters worse, even our war-time allies had begun to despise us: an opinion poll in the USA showed that 70 per cent of Americans were against further aid for the Brits.

It was into that gloomy scene that Brabazon came sailing along, brave, brave Brabazon and how Britain loved her! I'll never forget the summer they sent the Brab sweeping majestically and, it seemed, amazingly slowly along the South Coast on sunny afternoons so that holidaymakers could see for themselves how the taxpayers' money was being spent on this dizzy public project. A chorus of delight and ripples of applause followed her like a slipstream along coasts and headlands. She was marvellous to behold and the full, almost sweet roar of her eight Centaurus engines made everyone swell with pride. At last someone was *doing* something—and that someone was the Bristol Aeroplane Company with its colossal passenger plane. That would put us back on the map!

Aviation was a thrilling, magical world in those days. People, not computers, designed planes and, unlike computers, they came up with often wildly different shapes and designs, some excitingly novel. And, too, aviation was knocking on the door of an unknown, futuristic, even frightening world of greater and greater speed and more and more air travel. New planes were news and so were the men that flew them, the dashing test pilots...John Derry, the first Briton to break the sound barrier and the first in the world to smash it in a conventional jet, Neville Duke, whose terrifying supersonic bang dives in his egg-green Hawker Hunter were the sensation of the Farnborough Air Show and, in Bristol, A.J. 'Bill' Pegg, the man who flew the Brab.

Her story began at the end of 1942 when the Government set up a committee to examine the sort of planes British civil aviation would need once the war was over. The chairman was the aristocrat Lord Brabazon of Tara, who had been the first Englishman to pilot an aircraft. His committee suggested five types, ranging from a little taxi plane which was to become the successful de Havilland Dove to nothing less than the world's largest airliner, one which could carry 90 to 100 passengers non-stop from London to New York—a breathtakingly ambitious target in those days. The Bristol Aeroplane Company was chosen for this project and it was commissioned to build two planes, the experimental Brabazon I and a pre-production model, Brabazon II.

In charge of design was the brilliant Archibald Russell and his orders were to create an airliner which would rival the roomy luxury of great ocean liners like the *Queen Mary* and *Queen Elizabeth* on the lucrative transatlantic route. So Brab was, when you think about it, an aircraft conceived in the spirit of the elegant travel of 1930s ocean liners, built with 1940s aviation technology and aimed at a travelling public of the 1950s. The equation wasn't reassuring, but Russell pulled off an outstanding feat. He created a truly radical plane, a sleek, stream-lined, silver colossus of the air which was shockingly beautiful to a public which had become used to the aggressive functionalism of the big war-time bombers.

As the war ended, the Brab project gathered pace and size. Everything about it was huge and superlatives abounded. The plane's wingspan of 230 feet was identical to that of the American giant B-36 bombers, but Brab was

1951: The Brabazon I outside the Filton Assembly Hall.

just that little bit longer at 177 feet. The runway at Filton was specially extended from 1,500 yards to 2,750 yards and widened from 50 to 100 yards—and the village of Charlton partly razed in the process to noisy local protests—to accommodate Brab's running trials, making Filton the world's longest runway. A huge new aircraft assembly hall was built for constructing and servicing the Brabazon. Yes, that was the world's biggest too.

On the technical side, the project boasted any number of 'firsts', some of great significance. The Brab was, as Russell proudly pointed out afterwards, the world's first truly efficient aircraft structure and the plane incorporated such revolutionary systems as the first-ever fully powered controls. The plane was far too big to be controlled manually.

The Brabazon's initial customer was to be the British Overseas Airways Corporation, Britain's intercontinental airline, and BOAC were seen as the first of many operators for what the press called 'the prototype of the airliner of tomorrow'. Actually, her interior lay-out much more closely resembled the swish ocean liners of the past: a double-decker arrangement featuring a 32-seater cinema, cocktail bar, lounge for 32, First Class private bedrooms for 12, sleeping quarters of a less luxurious kind for 24.

Bill Pegg had flown more than 150 types of aircraft before he was given the job of testing the Brab, but nothing on this scale. He made a trip to Fort Worth in Texas to try his hand flying the B-36 and the huge 120-ton Convair C99 military transport to get the feel of flying on this scale. He was back in Bristol at the beginning of September, 1949.

Brabazon I made her maiden flight on Sunday September 5th, 1949 and Bristol's—well aware of the huge publicity value of their monster—let it be known that the first flight was imminent and invited 300 of the world's press to Filton to see the great event. As it happened, the flight came so unexpectedly that most of the press were caught unawares.

Pegg had spent the previous day trundling Brab up and down that immensely long runway and the most that the 10,000 or so spectators surrounding Filton airfield expected to see was a short 'hop' or two with Brabazon only just becoming airborne. Bill Pegg had other ideas. He liked the feel of the plane as he taxi-ed up to the Cribbs Causeway end of the runway and announced over the intercom to his nine fellow crew members: 'Boys, this is it. I am going to take her up right away.'

Bill Pegg swung the plane round, opened up the throttles and Brab ambled easily away. Her nose was up after 450 yards and 50 yards further along the runway she was up. Everyone cheered as the bright sunshine sparkled on her silver wings and fuselage as she climbed slowly over the Gloucester Road and cruised off towards Chipping Sodbury, making a five mile arc before a slow fly-past of Filton and then passing over Avonmouth and the northern suburbs of Bristol before returning for a smooth touch-down. Lord Brabazon was there to see it all for himself, standing in the control tower and smoking through a long cigarette holder. 'My faith has been justified' he said. 'I have never seen any trial go off so smoothly.'

Reginald Verdon-Smith, Bristol's joint managing director, was much more carried away. He took the microphone and called to Pegg in the cockpit: 'A splendid run! Well done!' Then he turned to Lord Brabazon and

Chief test pilot Bill Pegg at the controls of the giant Brabazon.

said excitedly: 'This will make a lot of chaps go gay today.'

It was a public relations triumph and messages of congratulations came pouring in from across the world. Bill Pegg was elevated to national hero. Mr Pegg treated the event rather more prosaically. He refused all offers of a celebration and drove home to have Sunday lunch with his family.

As the excitement died down, the more reflective executives at Bristol's must have taken a cooler look at the message from Sir Miles Thomas, chairman of BOAC. It read: 'The flight is the culmination of thousands of man-hours of faith, hope and effort on the part of technicians who have the courage to think big and look boldly to the future with typical enterprise.' All well and good, no doubt, but not a mention of BOAC's desire to get Brab into service. The publicity office at Filton thought overwise, issuing a press release describing a typical week in the working life of their giant.

Sunday:	*Depart* London Airport midnight (GMT)
Monday:	*Arrive* New York 0800 hrs (EST)
	Depart New York 1830 hrs (EST)
Tuesday:	*Arrive* London Airport 0800 hrs (GMT)
	Depart London Airport midnight (GMT)
Wednesday:	*Arrive* New York 0800 hrs (EST)
	Depart New York 1830 hrs (EST)
Thursday:	*Arrive* London Airport 0800 hrs (GMT)
	Depart London Airport midnight (GMT)
Friday:	*Arrive* New York 0800 hrs (EST)
	Depart New York 1830 hrs (EST)
Saturday:	*Arrive* London Airport 0800 hrs (GMT)

The press release continued: 'With three aircraft allotted to the route—two operating and one in reserve—seven services a week in each direction could be maintained. The degree of comfort provided by Brabazon merits special attention. It would be possible to leave London after a full evening's engagement, sleep throughout the crossing, and arrive in New York early the next morning, refreshed and ready for any business engagements. A day later, a passenger could be back in London. No intermediate stops with all passengers forced to leave the machine while re-fuelling takes place! A service giving speed with utmost comfort, an essential unit in the network of North Atlantic airlines.'

Ah dear, dreams, all dreams. The trouble with Brab, as Russell and his team were only too painfully aware as the months passed, was her lack of speed. She flew gracefully enough but very, very slowly, thanks to wings so thick a tall man could stand inside them and engines that hadn't the necessary beef. Her maiden flight was carried out at a pitiful 160 miles an hour, which isn't much faster than today's inter-city train services, and her planned cruising speed was a mere 250 miles an hour—and that at a time when jets were starting to get to grips with supersonic flight. It wasn't long before a new project, the Britannia, began to occupy Russell's time more than the Bristol Brabazon.

Brabazon's greatest moment was her maiden flight but she had a few more publicity successes to come, like the great welcome she received on a visit to

Brabazon's exceptional spaciousness well illustrated by this photograph of a corner of the passenger saloon.

London Airport and the excitement when she carried some passengers to Le Bourget airport in Paris. Bristol's rigged up some seats in the rear of that cavernous fuselage and carried visiting notables and airline representatives on short flips from Filton. All complimented the Brabazon on its smoothness, its quietness.

Brabazon II was never completed and in early 1952 it was announced that the project was to be cancelled. Brabazon I had completed about 400 hours of flying when the flight programme came to an end in September 1952. In a practical, significant gesture, Brabs I and II were quietly moved into a far corner of the great assembly hall to make way for the rising star the Britannia.

The world had changed, the Conservatives under Winston Churchill were back in power and no-one was surprised when, on Monday July 20th, 1953, the Minister of Supply, Duncan Sandys, announced to the House of Commons that the planes would be dismantled and sold for scrap, Mr Sandys said: 'The Brabazon II was intended to become the forerunner of a commercial type, but it has been superseded by the advent of the Comet and Britannia'. And some first-class American planes too, the airlines would have added.

The announcement led to criticisms. The lovely silver leviathan was derided as a 'costly white elephant' and it was pointed out that her £12 million development costs amounted to five bob from every man, woman and child in the country. The Bristol press were kinder and the *Evening Post*'s valedictory feature the next day was headlined regretfully: 'And So Farewell To The Great Might-Have-Been.' The Brabazon was consigned to the ranks of Great British Failures.

And yet . . . and yet . . . was Brabazon truly a failure? I don't think so at all. I believe we can be far kinder than critics, with their wisdom of hindsight, have been. I'll go further. I think there is a good case for arguing that the Brab, far from being one of the colossal failures of aviation history, was a resounding success.

Why? For a start, Britain desperately needed a postwar status symbol, a project to prove we were alive and kicking and back in business, and Brab certainly did that. She lifted morale, gave a new spring to the step and helped the British go forward into the 1950s with something to cheer about. For that alone, the Government's investment of £12 million seems justified.

The technical achievements were certainly there. The project gave Bristol's invaluable information about hydraulic systems, structural design, even metal fatigue. Physically, Brabazon's inheritance was a magnificent runway and assembly hall, legacies which have kept Bristol in the forefront of aviation ever since. And, of course, Brabazon helped to keep Bristol's aviation workforce intact immediately after the war.

By the time she was scrapped, Brabazon had done her job. Britain had begun to believe in itself again and there were new symbols, the Festival of Britain in 1951, the dawn of the Young Elizabethan age and, as the climax of goodbye to postwar austerity, the Coronation.

The Brab a failure?

Acker and All That Jazz

Roger Bennett on the great trad. boom

One rainy Saturday afternoon in the winter of 1952 my friend Otter took me out on his motor bike. Otter wasn't his real name: he was called Roger Davis, but we were in the 267th D.T.M. Scouts and we all had to have Woodcraft Names. Mine was Brock the Badger. We also had a Gannet and a Wolf and a Beaver and a Ricky and a Rocky and (because he came from Wiltshire) a White Horse, who wore tight leather shorts like a Swiss yodeller.

It was the first time I'd ever been on a motor bike and I was scared to death. But that wasn't the most significant feature of the journey.

We rode past Temple Meads, up over Totterdown, through Knowle and Whitchurch and out into the country. It was cold, wet, uncomfortable and exciting. No crash helmets, so dangerous too. But any motorised journey in those days, apart from the buses, was a rare treat. Nobody I knew had a car, not even Dad, though he did for a while ride an historic Francis Barnett motorbike my brother found on a farm, until one day it fell in half.

We swooped down Hursley Hill, up under the railway bridge, round to the left, down the hill under another railway bridge and into Pensford.

At the bottom of the hill, Otter alias Roger braked carefully to a halt. He parked the bike and we crossed the road to a drab little building on the corner with its name inscribed in stone: The Pensford Miners Welfare Institute. Roger pushed open the door and for the first time in my life I heard live jazz.

A woman with ginger hair sat knitting by a coal stove. A hairy man sat on a bicycle saddle fixed to a chromium stand, rapping at a primitive drumkit. A friend of Roger's called Onk sat plucking at a banjo.

In a semicircle in the middle of the room, three men sat alternately blowing instruments and dragging at cigarettes. A plump blond man like a big cherub played cheerful rasping noises on a tarnished trombone. A worried looking chap with a crewcut played jerky phrases on a trumpet which he kept on taking to pieces to examine the valves. And a stocky, tough-looking local with long sideboards and work-grimed fingers, pulled surprisingly attractive cascades of notes from a clarinet.

'Who's he?' I whispered.

'Acker Bilk' breathed my friend Otter.

'What's that?' 'It's his name.'

We sat enthralled as the newly formed Chew Valley Jazz Band rehearsed. I even remember the tunes. There was one called 'Tishomingo Blues', and another called 'Washington and Lee Swing'.

I think it must have been pretty rough, but it was still the most beautiful sound I had ever heard. The mushy Tin Pan Alley pop music of the time held no interest for me: but this was different.

'Will you teach me to play the clarinet please?' I asked Acker Bilk, wondering how a man got such a name. 'Too busy man,' said the leader with a grin, 'too busy', and he turned to talk to the ginger girl who later became Mrs Bilk.

Otter and I crept out, and I forgot to worry about the wet road and the bald tyres as I rode home on a cloud.

The next week, my friend Geoff Pugh lent me £7, and I went to the Arcade and bought an old clarinet with leaks and woodworm. Later I sold my Meccano to pay him back. Later again, I traded it in for a clarinet made of silver metal, which had been used in a Salvation Army band. Later again I saved up £20 and went to London and bought an ebonite instrument from Boosey and Hawkes. Finally I swapped this with my friend Ray for an old Selmer which I still play to this day.

We had discovered jazz more or less by accident, my friends Geoff and Wayne and I. They were always a bit flashier and better off in those days (in fact I think they still are), and they used to go to Charles H. Lockier's Sunday Pop Concerts at the Embassy Cinema. The Colston Hall was still being rebuilt after its latest fire.

One Sunday the band was Harry Gold and his Pieces of Eight, playing a sort of tidied up Dixieland. Geoff and Wayne came home much impressed, and specially taken with a tune called 'Ory's Creole Trombone'.

We didn't know what an Ory or a Creole was, but we went to Allen's record shop on Gloucester Road to ask. Geoff had a gramophone. It was a wind-up machine in the attic, and its volume control was a pair of wooden doors you opened or closed. Before we discovered jazz, we used to put pieces of paper on the turntable and paint patterns of circles and spirals as it whirled round at approximately 78 revolutions per minute.

Anyway, Allens produced their Parlophone catalogue, and couldn't find a Harry Gold version of our tune. But there was one by someone called Louis Armstrong and his Hot Seven. It cost five shillings and we had to wait a fortnight for it to come in. Then we took it back to Geoff's attic in Sommerville Road, St Andrew's Park, and listened spellbound. The next weekend we went back to Allens with Geoff's pocket money and ordered 'Doctor Jazz' by Jelly Roll Morton.

The others then got hold of a book by Rudi Blesh called *Shining Trumpets* which gave an earnest though rather narrow-minded version of the beginnings of jazz, and told us which records to listen to.

Geoff and Wayne, thoroughly bitten by the bug, found there was a jazz band in Bristol called the Avon Cities. It was many months before I got permission to go with them. I was a very obedient lad. But eventually I was

Roger Bennett is the clarinettist on the right.

allowed to stay out late and visit the fleshpots of Great George Street.

We caught the Number 21 to the Centre and joined a generally bearded and duffel-coated procession up Park Street and round the corner to the Y.W.C.A. through the side door, up the garden path (lit by candles in jam jars) to a faintly oriental summerhouse-cum-tennis-pavilion, housing the smoky but strictly non-alcoholic New Orleans Jazz Club.

The Avons were led then, as now, by a gaunt trumpet player called Geoff Nichols, whose brother Peter writes quite good plays. I remembered seeing them from afar and several forms below at Bristol Grammar School. There was also a trombone player called Diz, and two clarinet players, Butch and Mike. I liked the way Mike played and with incredible cheek repeated the request which had met with no success at Pensford.

Certainly, said Mike Hitchings. He'd help me to learn the clarinet. And in an old Citroen like Maigret's, he'd drive every week to our house in St Andrew's Park, and spend a couple of hours patiently coaching me through 'Cakewalkin' Babies' and 'Chicago Buzz' for no more reward than a cup of coffee and a Marie biscuit.

By this time, Wayne had conned an old banjo out of a girl friend's uncle, and Geoff had amassed a huge collection of sheet music of jazz classics for piano, mostly boogie-woogie and Jelly Roll Morton. We began rehearsing, if you can call it that, in the front room of Geoff's house, or rather his parents' house, in Sommerville Road. It was awful. And the better we got the louder we got, so eventually we began hiring The Foundry.

The Foundry was one of a series of jazz pubs which were demolished to make way for the new age of superstores and super highways. In fact the Old Duke in King Street has the distinction of being the only Bristol pub I've played in regularly which hasn't been demolished. Yet.

The Foundry was in Newfoundland Road, and I think we paid five shillings for the use of the upstairs room to rehearse. Like all pub clubrooms, it was decked out with bison horns and framed portraits of worthy gentlemen in aprons who were leading members of the Royal Antedeluvian Order of Buffaloes. I never met a Buffalo who liked jazz or a jazzman who was a Buffalo, but the two together helped to sustain many a backstreet pub in the fifties.

We began rehearsing at the Foundry and soon recruited a ginger haired trombone player called Pete Dyer. He had a car and was socially a cut above us; possibly several cuts. He announced that his father owned most of the vinegar in England.

Next to the Foundry was Purnells Vinegar Works, later purchased for some reason by the *Daily Express*, and Pete proved his unlikely claim by taking us in after rehearsal one night, showing us the giant vats bubbling in the darkness, and handing us all armfuls of bottles of vinegar.

After a few weeks, Mum, her larder full of vinegar, pleaded with me not to bring home any more.

Eventually we were ready for public performance. Well we weren't, but in those days you could get away with murder. We called ourselves the Vieux Carre Jazz Band (a name we culled from *Shining Trumpets*), and appeared first at Acker's pub, the Crown and Dove, and then, very nervously, at the Y.W.C.A. summerhouse in Great George Street.

Public appearances were rare. Most of the time was spent in endless, stumbling, groping rehearsals. At the Foundry: the Lamb and Anchor in Milk Street (both now gone). The Earl Russell in Lawrence Hill. The King David at the bottom of St Michael's Hill. Any pub with a piano, however awful, and they usually were.

Then I got a message from Bath. Somebody called Terry Lightfoot had left, so would I play for Joe Brickell's jazz club at the Club Dixie?

They paid me five shillings, and I think the train fare was 4s 6d, but I didn't drink and the sixpence was clear profit. The club was in a Nissen hut somewhere near the station. I said yes, and at last I was in a real band.

Joe played, and indeed still does, in the style of Nat Gonella, with his head on one side, one eye half closed, and a filthy old beret hung over the bell of his trumpet as a mute.

It was a great experience. But after being dumped one night at Bath Spa station after a wearying expedition to Cheltenham and having to wait three frozen hours for the milk train to Temple Meads and the walk home, I'd had enough.

Joe's pianist Gerry Bath and I left, to form the Climax Jazz Band.

Gerry appeared to be sewn permanently into the same Fair Isle pullovers.

! JAZZ AT THE CIVIC !

THE WESTERN JAZZ FEDERATION PRESENTS

ANOTHER TERRIFIC

SATURDAY NIGHT SESSION

with *Two Jazz Bands*

RANDY BARTLETT
And His Jazz Group

GERRY   BATH'S
Climax Jazz Band

Plus !   Compere

DAVE VARNEY

Star of "Rave with Dave" Fame

COLLEGE   GREEN   CIVIC   RESTAURANT

(Bristol)

SATURDAY, OCTOBER 13th, 7.30-11 p.m.

TICKETS 3/- from STANS, 5, Denmark St.
BROWNS, St. Stephens Street (MEMBERS 2/-)
or 4/6 at door (If available)

Denny Bros., Printers, Bury St. Edmunds

His friend Brian played the banjo, and we were very pleased because he always brought his wife, who had a marvellous figure and wore very tight sweaters. I recruited a fellow Bristol Grammar School boy called Mark Burnham, not because he knew anything about jazz but because he had a trombone. Luckily he caught on very quickly.

Our first trumpet player was a territorial army officer called Bob Jones, who played jazz with slightly military overtones. Years later I was riding my Vespa over the Cotswolds when he appeared in front of me out of a ditch, covered in camouflage and carrying a rifle. 'Sorry old chap,' he said. 'Can't stop. We're advancing.' He climbed over a wall and disappeared.

Bob was later replaced by my friend Oz, who was a student teacher at Redland College. I would go there and queue up in the canteen with him to get free cups of tea. On one memorable occasion we played in the college hall to illustrate a lecture entitled 'Humphrey Lyttelton: His Life And Times.'

The Climax Jazz Band had been going for a year or so, with appearances at various village halls and student functions, when we decided we were ready to contribute something to the recorded history of music, so we asked Stan to record us.

Stan Strickland, who later moved upmarket to tapes and CDs and so forth, had a little record shop in Denmark Street opposite Blakes Medical Stores. There was another similar shop underneath Stan's: and both attracted a somewhat furtive class of customer. So to make it clear that we were not after certain items of a personal nature, we would walk very loudly and positively up the middle of the road, and then wheel left and clatter noisily up Stan's stairs.

The earliest jazz record shop had been run, first at Christmas Steps and then in Horfield Road by an extraordinary character called Tiki Daniel, who had a goatlike beard, long yellow fingers, a very long camel hair overcoat and a Messerschmitt bubble car. He always seemed to do a lot of talking but not much business. Stan took on his role, but in a more commercial way. Not only were the records more organised, but he invested in a machine which could make L.P. discs.

It didn't press them in any quantity. It carved them out one at a time from acetate, producing great billowing piles of black swarf. Every record took as long to make as it did to play, so it was a laborious process. I still have precious copies of our first discs but they have gone a sort of green colour and they crackle and hiss a lot.

Stan first recorded us in the shop, with the band dotted around the place to achieve some sort of balance. I had to sit out on the stairs.

Later his technique became more sophisticated, and we made a memorable record in the Walter Baker Memorial Hall, St George. The session took some time because we first had to lift the piano on to a very high stage and it took at least an hour to get our breath back. Then Stan lost his headphones, so all communication was done with violent semaphore signals from the back room.

I suppose it had been much the same in New Orleans.

All this time we had to rely on the Avon Cities and the Chew Valley bands for leadership (unless you were a modernist in which case you went to the

Roost in Old Market). It was bit like City and Rovers and the Rugby. Not many supporters went to more than one.

We yearned to hear the men in the pages of *Shining Trumpets* before they died. And eventually the musicians unions of Britain and America managed to thrash out an agreement which released first a trickle and later a flood of the greats to appear at our concert halls and clubs.

The *Evening Post's* municipal and speedway correspondent Jim Webber organised a trip to the Empress Hall in London to see Louis Armstrong. We had to change seats to give way to Princess Margaret. Louis appeared on a revolving stage with a one-legged tap dancer called Peg Leg Bates. A bizarre show, but the emotional experience of seeing possibly the greatest ever jazz musician brought lumps to our throats.

Later Louis came to the Colston Hall, as did Bechet, Ellington, Basie, Hines, Teagarden, Hawkins . . . all the surviving greats of jazz. At last we began to understand what it was really all about.

I escaped from National Service after two months because of my feet. The *Evening Post* got its own back by posting me to Stroud. I couldn't find any jazz, so I used to strap my clarinet and soprano sax on the back of the Vespa and scoot through rain, fog, ice and snow to Bristol once a week to blow with the newly-formed Blue Notes at the Ship in Redcliff Hill. (Yes they pulled that down as well, but not until the sixties).

The landlord Ron Wallington diagnosed us as 'A Nice Class Of Kiddy' so he let us stay despite dark forebodings from the superintendent at Bedminster Police Station.

The trouble, when it came, came from elsewhere.

The Teddy Boys would invade jazz events like the parents evening at Hengrove Scout Hut. Tables were upturned and dinner plates flew through the air. A brave scout leapt in the air and in the manner of Peter Shilton tipped one flying plate over my head, saving me from severe injury. It hit the drummer instead.

Fights broke out at Filwood Community Centre, and at The Civic Restaurant on College Green. In the Chicago tradition, we kept playing as chaos reigned.

But times were changing. Rock and Roll had arrived. And suddenly the jazz bands were no longer the expression of rebellious youth.

The sixties had arrived, and *we* were the old fogeys.

BRISTOL
EVENING POST
No. 4,118—1½d. The Paper All Bristol Asked For and Helped to Create Thur., July 26 1945

Labour Party Secures Its First Working Majority in Commons

		Returned	Gains	Losses	Net Gains	Net Losses	†At the Dissolution
201	CONS. - -	187	7	175	—	168	358
	NAT. - -	1	—	1	—	1	9
	LIB. NAT. -	13	1	15	—	14	27
391	LAB. - -	367	202	4	198	—	163
	LIB. - -	10	3	10	—	7	19
	I.L.P - -	3	—	—	—	—	3
	COMMUNISTS	2	1	—	1	—	1
	C. WEALTH	1	—	1	—	1	3
	INDS. & Others*	8	2	10	—	8	24

*Including Ind. Con., Ind. Progressive, Ind. Nat., Ind. Lib., Scottish Nationalist, Welsh Nationalist, Republican.
†Seven seats were vacant and there are 25 new seats.

Total Returned: 592 out of 627.

FORECAST OF THE NEW CABINET

SIR S. CRIPPS AT HOME OFFICE?

LABOUR HAS SECURED A WORKING MAJORITY IN THE HOUSE OF COMMONS FOR THE FIRST TIME IN HISTORY.

AMONG the Ministers who have lost their seats in the change-over are:

Sir James Grigg (War), Mr. Bracken (Admiralty), Mr. Macmillan (Air), Mr. Amery (India), Mr. Lloyd (Information), Mr. Mabane (Secretary of State), Mr. Law (Education), Mr. Hore-Belisha (Social Insurance), Sir D. Somervell (Home Office), Mr. Sandys (Works), Mr. Ernest Brown (Aircraft Production), and Sir W. Womersley (Pensions).

In the new Woodford Division Mr. Churchill had a 17,200 majority, although his Independent opponent polled 10,488 votes. Mr. Eden has also been elected.

On the Labour side, Mr. Attlee, Mr. Bevin, Mr. Morrison, Mr Alexander, Mr. Greenwood, Sir S. Cripps, and Mr. Dalton were among the earliest to be returned.

Sir Archibald Sinclair and Sir William Beveridge were beaten by Conservatives, the former by a margin of six. Of the first 22 of the new divisions, Labour won 14 and the Conservatives eight.

PARTY CHIEF LOSES SEAT

FULL RESULTS START IN SUPPLEMENT

WHILE the results were streaming in, the King carried out his normal State duties at Buckingham Palace, writes the Press Association Lobby correspondent.

Roughly, Labour appeared to be winning two seats out of every three, and as early as 1.45 p.m. it was certain that the Opposition parties had a majority in the new House.

That raised the question whether Mr. Churchill would decide to resign the Premiership at once—possibly by going to see the King tonight—or whether he will defer resignation, as he is entitled to do, until the House meets.

Speculation also began about the possible composition of a Labour Cabinet, with Mr. Attlee as Prime Minister. Holders of key posts might include:

Mr. Ernest Bevin (Foreign Secretary).
Mr. Herbert Morrison (Chancellor of the Exchequer).
Sir Stafford Cripps (Home Secretary).
Mr. Hugh Dalton (Board of Trade).
Sir William Jowitt (National Insurance).
Mr. Arthur Greenwood (Health).

Back Page, Col. 1.

The Electors' Choice

BRISTOL'S FIVE M.P.S

BRISTOL'S new M.P.s are as follows:—

CENTRAL: Ald. S. Awbery (Lab.).
NORTH: Mr. W. Coldrick (Lab.).
SOUTH: Coun. W. A. Wilkins (Lab.).
EAST: Sir Stafford Cripps (Lab.).
WEST: Col. Oliver Stanley (C.).

Mr. N. F. Newsome (L.), former [illegible] journalist, failed to secure [illegible] at Penryn. Lt.-Col. Alan [illegible] (C.) had a majority of 2,619 [illegible] Lee, who unsuccessfully

Back Page, Col. 2.

LABOUR GAINS

FROM CONS.

Hulme, Manchester
Exchange, Manchester
Salford South
Edge Hill, Liverpool
Moss Side, Manchester
Stockton-on-Tees
Northampton
Lincoln
Salford N.
Salford W.
Hammersmith S.
Exchange, Liverpool
Blackley, Manchester
Sheffield Central
Grimsby
Duddeston, Birmingham
Tynemouth
Kirkdale, Liverpool
Peterborough, Northampton
Birkenhead W.
Bristol Central
Mitcham, Surrey
Accrington
Paddington N.
Gloucester
Dulwich, Camberwell
Fairfield, Liverpool
Birmingham W.
Deritend, Birmingham
Wolverh'pton W.
Eccles
Drake Div., Plymouth
Walton, Liverpool
Lewisham W.
Yardley, Birmingham
Leeds Central
Sutton, Plymouth
York
Camberwell N.W.
Aston, Birmingham
Warrington
Fulham East
Kettering, Northampton
Dudley
Bilston, Wolverhampton
Chorley, Lancs.
King's Lynn
Carlisle
Cardiff Central
Sparkbrook, Birmingham
Battersea S.
Ladywood, Birmingham
Woolwich West
Clitheroe, Lancs
St. Pancras N.
Wimbledon
Leeds, N.E.
Preston (2 seats)
Buckingham, Bucks
Greenwich
Kensington N.
Dover
Hull N.W.
Swindon
Bootle
Willesden E.
Brentford and
Louth, Lincs.
St. Pancras S.E.
Brixton, Lambeth
Rossendale
Halifax
Darlington
Widnes
Cambridge
Buckrose (Yorks East Riding)
Lowestoft
Portsmouth Cen
Smethwick
Hull South-West
Norfolk South
Portsmouth Nth.
St. Pancras S.W
Wallsend
Balham and Tooting
Bradford E.
Erdington, Birmingham
Lewisham East
Sowerby (Yorks
Norfolk S.W.
West Riding)
Colchester (Essex
Ilford North
Norwood (Lambeth)
Cardiff South
Clapham (Wandsworth)
Islington East
Leeds West
Derby
Acton (Middlesex)
Hendon North (Middlesex)
Walthamstow E.
Wansbeck (Northumberl'd)
Elland (Yorks West Riding)
East Ham North
Ilford North
Kings' Norton, Birmingham
Nottingham Cen
Essex (South-Eastern)
Taunton
Newcastle Cen.
Maidstone (Kent)
Berwick and Haddington
The Wrekin, Salop
Epping (Essex)
Wycombe, Bucks
Sudbury, Suffolk
Stafford
Leicester S.
Crewe
Rushcliffe, Notts
Bedford, Beds.
Cambridgeshire
Burton, Staffs.
Nottingham E.
Hackney N.
Bradford N.
Derbyshire S.
Norwich
Heywood & Radcliffe, Lancs
Stoke Newington
Leyton
Barrow-in-Furness
Glasgow, Kelvingrove
Leicester E.
Hitchin, Herts.
Rusholme, Manchester
Lanark N.
Llandaff & Barry
Spelthorne, Middlesex
Coventry W.
Fairfield, Liverpool
Lanark, Lanarkshire
Stalybridge and Hyde
Leicester E.
Belper, Derby
Stourbridge, Worcs.
Stroud, Glos.
Winchester, Hants
Enfield, Middlesex
St. Alban's, Hertford
Rutherglen, Lanark
Newport
Edinburgh N.
Croydon S.
Rochester
Hitchin
Barrow-in-Furness
Chislehurst, Kent
Faversham
Gillingham, Rochester
Yorks N. Riding
Hartlepools
Bolton (2 seats)
Watford
Dundee
Newcastle W.
Stretford, Lancs.
Blackburn (2 seats)
Gravesend
Edinburgh Cen.
Norfolk N.
Kidderminster
Wellingborough, Northampton
Penryn and Falmouth
Sunderland

FROM NAT.

Devonport, Plymouth
Bradford S.
Huddersfield
Spen Valley
Norwich
Walsall
Kilmarnock, Ayr & Bute
Gateshead
Sunderland
Reading
Bristol North
Luton, Beds.
Cardiff E.
Motherwell, Lanark
Bosworth, Leicestershire
Leicester W.
Newcastle E.

FROM LIBS.

Bethnal Green S.W.
Middlesbro' W.
Dundee
Birkenhead E.
Wolverh'pton E.
Leith

FROM IND.

Eye, Suffolk
Derbyshire W.
Maldon, Essex

CON. GAINS

FROM IND.

Wallasey
Maldon, Essex

FROM COM. WEALTH

Skipton, Yorks.

FROM LAB.

Isle of Ely

FROM LIBS.

Berwick-on-Tweed
Carnarvon Dist.
Caithness and Sutherland
Barnstaple

LIB. GAINS

FROM LAB.

Carmarthen
Dorset N.

The British Military Govt., which took over control of the Austrian city of Graz on Tuesday, has announced an increase in the bread ration, said the Austrian radio today.

OTHER GAINS

Hammersmith N.
Great Yarmouth
Eddisbury, Galloway
Swansea West
Mile End Stepney
Ormskirk

Majority of Four

Group-Capt. the Hon. Geo. Ward (C.), was returned for Worcester with a majority of four after three recounts.

There were also three recounts at Rusholme, Manchester, where Mr. H. J. Hutchinson (Lab.), finally had a majority of 10. The first recount gave Maj. F. W. Cundiff, retiring Con. member, an apparent majority.

More than 100 Germans have been convicted for violating the 9.30 p.m. curfew in Wiesbaden, Luxembourg radio reported today.

"GRATIFYING"

MR. ATTLEE ON THE RESULTS

Mr. Attlee commenting this afternoon on the fact that this is the first time in the history of the country that Labour has had a clear majority, said: "It will enable us to implement the policy of the Socialist Party.

"It is a very remarkable and gratifying result which shows that the electorate will respond to a clear and definite policy based on principles and on the application of those principles to the needs of the present day."

THUNDERSTORMS

S.W. England: Dull, with periods of thundery rain and scattered thunderstorms, fair tonight; rather cool.

Further Outlook: Mainly fair.

Lighting-up: 10.8 p.m. to 4.24 a.m.

By-elections Necessary

DEAD MEN AT TOP OF POLL

Two dead men headed the poll in their constituencies — Bromley and Monmouth — this afternoon, and a by-election will be necessary at each place.

THEY were Sir Edward Campbell and Mr. Leslie R. Pym, who had retained the seats for the Conservative Party.

For the first time in electoral history, the overwhelming majority of the votes polled in a general election were today counted simultaneously.

The only exceptions were the University seats and Central Hull, numbering eight divisions and returning 13 members.

Until after the last war, both voting and counting were spread over a number of days, and in more recent elections the declarations were made on two days.

Special arrangements were agreed to well before the break-up of the Coalition to delay the count to enable Service votes from Europe and the Far East to be included.

The Lucky Three

The next House of Commons will consist of 640 members, 25 new divisions having been formed by the carving-up of old constituencies with exceptionally heavy electorates.

The names of three M.P.s were known before the count began—Mr. Will John (Lab., W. Rhondda), Mr. D. G. Logan (Lab., Scotland Div., Liverpool), and Sir William Allen (C., Armagh) having been returned unopposed.

The election in Central Hull was delayed owing to the death of the former M.P. after his nomination as a candidate, and the counting there will not take place till Aug 9.

In the seven University divisions, returning 12 members, the declarations will take place on various dates within the next week. The results are expected from the Universities of Oxford, London, Wales, and Belfast on Monday, from Cambridge on Tuesday, from the Combined English Universities (including Bristol) on Wednesday, and from Scottish Universities on Thursday.

Declarations were thus due today in 609 constituencies, returning 624 members.

The total electorate for England and Wales, Scotland and N. Ireland is 33,126,546.

Fun and Fellowship

The post war political scene fondly recalled by former Bristol MP Lord Cocks of Hartcliffe

On July 26th, 1945 my father met me at Temple Meads Station with the words 'Churchill's ploughed his exams'. Thus I learnt of the Labour landslide returning Attlee's Government with a huge majority. Polling Day had been on July 5th, but the counting was delayed while the votes of millions of servicemen and women abroad were brought back to this country.

Winston Churchill himself came to Bristol on April 21st, 1945 where he received the Freedom of the City and later as Chancellor of Bristol University conferred Honorary Degrees on Ernest Bevin and A. V. Alexander. Both had strong Bristol connections, Alexander's sisters keeping a corset shop on the Triangle at one time. Ernest Bevin's early working days were spent in Bristol, and as late as the early 1970s, I used to talk to an old man in his 90s who frequented The Venture on Melvin Square and who used to work on the B. & P. lemonade wagon with Ernie Bevin. Sir Stafford Cripps should also have received a Degree but refused at the last minute because of slighting remarks made about him by Churchill. Churchill himself had a great regard for Bristol, praising the enterprise of its Burghers and giving his name to the Winston Club, the top Debating Society in the University.

The landslide was reflected in the Bristol results. Sir Stafford Cripps, Member for Bristol East since 1931, was returned with a majority of 17,902—although he had only been reconciled with the Labour Party just before the General Election, following his disagreement which went back to the pre-war period. In Bristol Central Lady Apsley, confined to a wheelchair following an accident, was displaced by Stan Awbery, a dockworkers' official from Barry. He was later nick-named 'The Question Master' by the local papers because of his constant interrogation of Ministers in the Commons. Lady Apsley herself had succeeded her husband on his death in 1943.

The electoral truce had been broken in Bristol Central and a by election fought, when Jenny Lee had stood as Independent, helped by supporters of the Commonwealth Party, which for a short time had a Literature Shop in Cotham Hill. Notable speakers in her support included Tom Driberg, Michael Foot and Hannen Swaffer.

In Bristol North, Will Coldrick gained the seat for Labour from J. H. Britton (Liberal National), Managing Director of the Kingswood boot & shoe firm. Will Coldrick, a former miners' agent in Monmouthshire became President of the Bristol Co-operative Society in 1942 and lived in Sea Mills. In Bristol South, W. A. Wilkins maintained Labour's grip on the seat, succeeding A. G. Walkden, who had won the seat for Labour in 1935. Will, my predecessor, was President of the Bristol branch of the Typographical Association, a city councillor and worked for the old *Evening World* newspaper.

The sole Conservative in Bristol was Col. Oliver Stanley, elected in Bristol West. He was a man of wide Ministerial experience, who had represented Westmoreland since 1924 until the Dissolution of Parliament. The former Conservative Member, C.T. Culverwell, retired under a cloud following some remarks in a speech to the effect that 'we ought to be siding with Hitler against the Russians, rather than fighting him'.

The General Election landslide was repeated in the local election results of Thursday, November 1st, 1945. This seems a strange time to have local elections, accustomed as we are to May, but it was changed soon afterwards for the present timing by the Representation of The People Act, 1948. This entailed Charlie Gill doing an extra six months as Lord Mayor.

Labour gained nine seats which with the customary Aldermanic adjustments, gave Labour a majority of 24. Labour was back in with a majority for the first time since 1937, when they had a majority of six.

The occupations of the successful Labour candidates make very interesting reading, particularly when they are compared with current trends. Four trade union officials, including one retired, a snuff blender, four housewives, a retired school mistress, insurance agent, shop fitter, dentist, Bristol Co-operative agent, G.P.O. overseer, tailor, postal worker, political agent, railway fireman, two engine drivers, railway claims inspector, Sgt. Royal Marines, Cpl. Essex Regiment, letterpress printer, coal depot foreman.

These were people of wide experience, not only of the pre-war conditions of deprivation, but also of the ravages of wartime and an understanding of the massive reconstruction job that was needed.

All these people were dedicated, and believed passionately in what they were doing, receiving no financial rewards in terms of allowances etc. Indeed, many were well out of pocket over the years because of their support of Labour, often walking miles to attend meetings because they could not afford the bus or tram fare.

It must be said that their opponents were also dedicated to the well-being of Bristol, but there were few who were in straitened circumstances, as they represented more the business and professional side of Bristol. The opponents stood as Citizen candidates. The Citizen Party was created in the mid 1920s, said to be uniting all anti-Socialist elements, although to my mind towards the end, only the late Alderman E. W. Byrt, a Liberal, could be identified as not a Conservative. In 1956, the late Claude Taylor broke cover and came forward as a Conservative candidate, although he later withdrew. It was not until 1973 that the Tories eventually came clean, and stood as Conservatives under their own colours. Having lived through pre-war and

Sir Stafford Cripps MP for Bristol East won a resounding victory in the Labour landslide in 1945. He held the seat from 1931 until 1950.

war years, they were equally conscious of the need to re-build and expand the city, although obviously there were philosophical differences as to how this should be done.

The Labour Group met the day after the Local Elections, and re-appointed Arthur Parish as Leader, with G. A. Watson Allan as his Deputy and Percy Raymond as Whip.

Arthur Parish was an immensely able man, but above all, he was a superb chairman, able to control debates and draw meetings to decisions at the right time. His colleagues were also very gifted, often having had little formal education. Many were immensely knowledgeable, often self-taught and building up their own libraries. One such was Harry Hennessey, sometimes known as the stormy petrel, but more often as 'the poor man's lawyer', holding interviews at Old Market and doing his best to help everyone who came there. It was not unknown for Harry to go and squat on the front doorstep when a family, faced with eviction, was expecting the bailiffs. Helen Strimer, later Helen Bloom, had a tireless record of service on all health matters. Her sisters, Mrs Sacof and Mrs Britton, also made a great contribution being both councillors and pillars of the local Fabian Society.

The Citizens Party was led by Sir John Inskip, who had worked very closely with Arthur Parish on the Emergency Committee set up to run the war situation in Bristol.

Some of the Council agenda items after the war would bemuse young people today. For example, in November, 1946 Alderman Havergal Downes Shaw asked why '18 months after the end of hostilities in Europe, a very large area of the Downs were still surrounded by barbed wire and entrance by the public forbidden'. In June, 1947 Alderman Alf Duggan asked 'if a man buys his Anderson shelter can he put it on his allotment—if not, why not?'. Queries were also raised about the demolition of static water tanks. The reply was 251 had gone and 119 remained. At the same time Governors were appointed to Winsley Sanatorium. This T.B. Sanatorium near Limpley Stoke has fortunately long been used for other purposes. Pig bins are also mentioned, because with food shortage there was a constant struggle to find land to grow more vegetables and save food for feeding livestock. In these days, when there is much talk of morality in politics, most people do not realise that the post-war Labour Government introduced bread rationing to divert grain to India where famine was rife. Bread was not even rationed during the War, yet the Labour Government was prepared to face unpopularity because of the desperate needs of others overseas.

Young couples struggling to get a house today, will be envious of a reply given to a question about purchase of council houses: 'the Council grants loans to buy private dwellings with a maximum repayment period of 30 years with interest ranging from 1¾%-2¾%.'

Housing was the greatest problem the Council faced. The slum clearance programme, coupled with the number of houses destroyed or severely damaged during the blitz, meant that drastic measures were needed. Charlie Gill, as Chairman of the Housing Committee, provided the drive required, and the Council minutes record a series of massive compulsory purchase orders to acquire the necessary land, which were un-opposed by the Citizen

Party, who fully recognised the need. For example, on April 13th, 1948 the purchase of 585 acres on the southern slopes of Dundry was authorised to build the Hartcliffe and Withywood Estates. On June 15th, 1948, 60 acres were purchased at Manor Farm. The same minutes mention the building of the Northern Storm Water Interceptor—unfortunately the Southern Malago Storm Water Interceptor was opened only in the 1970s. Had it been built sooner, South Bristol would have escaped the disastrous 1968 floods. So successful was the house building programme that during the 1956 local elections Jack Radnedge, President of the Borough Labour Party, writing on its behalf in the *Evening Post*, was able to boast that Labour had laid out seven great estates since the end of the war.

In recent years it has become fashionable to criticize these large estates, and no doubt with hindsight more community facilities could have been incorporated, but at the time they were built, the over-riding need was to put roofs over heads. Just how much was done is shown by figures given in reply to a question by Ted Bishop in November, 1950.

	Corporation	Private	Total
Houses completed	9,959	1,315	11,272
Houses building	2,667	348	3,015

Since the end of the War.

Education was the other great priority problem and with equal foresight the Council acquired sites for a ring of schools circling Bristol to serve the new estates. Reg Cunningham was Chairman of the Education Committee, then Ald. F. C. Williams, followed by John St. John Reade. St. John Reade had been dismissed by Clifton College, where he was a schoolmaster, for standing for the City Council, and was very upset, particularly when later the Chaplain of Clifton College, The Rev. Peter Brooke, was allowed to take his seat as a Councillor for the other side without any quibble.

St. John Reade was a man of immense understanding, humanity and commonsense. I remember at an Education Committee Meeting in the late 1950s, his weary comment on being presented with yet another set of statistics of juvenile offenders; 'in my youth, if the policeman caught us doing anything wrong, he used to give us a good clip with his gloves and send us home—now they would open a file on each of us!' The first of the new secondary schools were opened at Hengrove and Lockleaze in 1954. I applied to each for a job, but was, as usual, turned down.

There were party disputes about the role of the grammar schools, direct grant places and other matters, but the basic drive to build schools to cater for the rising school population was unimpeded. On reflection, I think too much was expected of the comprehensive system too soon. Standards and values take years to establish, but now the achievements of Bristol schools reflect great credit on the spadework done at this time. Bristol's special schools owe a great debt to Ald. Mrs. Florence Brown, Bristol's first woman Lord Mayor.

A great deal of the planning and re-building of the Centre of Bristol was also done with inter party co-operation and again—although hindsight criticizes some decisions—at the time, and on all available advice, the right things were done.

How was it that two groups of councillors with such different backgrounds were able to make such progress so rapidly? I discussed this with The Rt. Rev. Mervyn Stockwood, formerly Bishop of Southwark, who as Vicar of Matthew Moorfields, and a Labour councillor, was in the thick of things at this time. He traced it back to the relationship established between Arthur Parish and Sir John Inskip through their work on the Emergency Committee. Not only had they worked very closely together, but latterly, John Inskip mellowed and quite exceptionally the Labour Council made him a Freeman of the City.

There were also opportunities for councillors to meet on an informal all-party basis through the Christian Group. This Group met for a Church Service before every council meeting in Christchurch with holy communion held twice a year in the Lord Mayor's Chapel, St. Ewen. During Lent meetings were held in the Lord Mayor's Parlour under the Chairmanship of the Bishop of Bristol, to discuss topics of general interest unrelated to any specific items on a council agenda. Discussion could, therefore, range freely without being tied to specific group decisions. Topics would include education, housing, planning and the welfare of young people, constructive use of their free time and training in citizenship. In these days of vandalism and hooliganism, it is incredible to record that throughout the war, every Church was left open because of the need for immediate access in fire bomb raids, yet there was not one reported case of theft or desecration throughout this time. The Christian Group also organised occasional services on the Downs and in the Colston Hall, which were packed out.

Political opponents, although they differed, respected each other and forged friendships which lasted over the years. In a way, it could be described as the local equivalent of Butskellism (the phrase given to the closeness of the views on many topics of R. A. Butler and Hugh Gaitskell).

In case this all seems too cosy, there were political differences and party sniping such as when in December 1947, Sir John Inskip put down a motion complaining about Alderman Hennessey allowing Bristol Borough Labour Party to hold a Carnival in St. George's Park. Labour's Whip, Percy Raymond, moved an amendment, which was accepted by all—a 'Usual Channels' solution if ever I saw one. Again, in 1947 George Ford complained about an unauthorised street collection taken for the Labour Party during the May Day Procession on Sunday May 4th.

It should also be remembered that Bristolians were bound together by their wartime experiences when Bristol had been subjected to repeated damaging air raids by the Luftwaffe.

Nationally, Bristol went into the 1950 General Election with six constituencies, following re-distribution. Stan Awbery, Stafford Cripps, Oliver Stanley and Will Wilkins were returned for Bristol Central, South East, West and South respectively. The Conservative candidate in Bristol Central was· John Peyton, later M.P. for Yeovil and a prominent Parliamentarian, both in the Commons and, latterly, the Lords. Will Coldrick won the new North East seat and Lt. Commdr. Gurney Braithwaite

Winston Churchill signing the Roll of Freemen after receiving the freedom of the city.

was elected Conservative for the new North West.

Sir Stafford Cripps was already ailing when he was re-elected and retired soon afterwards. He was a giant of a man, a devout Christian, respected across all Parties and made a great contribution to the country during and after the war. I myself heard him preach once in St. Michael's, Alderman F.C. Vyvyan Jones' church, and it made a lasting impression on me. The by-election threw up a new labour M.P., Anthony Wedgwood Benn. A protegee of Roy Jenkins and Tony Crosland, he had beaten the local favourite at the selection conference and represented the seat until the death of his father, Viscount Stansgate. He then fought his titanic struggle to renounce his peerage, including two by-elections against the Conservative candidate, Malcolm St Clair. He is a man of exceptional gifts, a highly original thinker, and spell binding orator. Nowadays his name is associated with extreme views, but in those days, things were very different. Many of his early questions and contributions in Parliament were on colonial matters, as he was closely associated with the Movement for Colonial Freedom. It is not possible to talk about Bristol East without mentioning Herbert Rogers, a seemingly indestructible Labour stalwart, now in his 90s, who has served the

party in Bristol East through thick and thin for more years than anybody can remember.

Another vacancy occurred in 1951 in Bristol West with the death of Oliver Stanley. Sir Walter Monckton was returned as Conservative member to continue a distinguished career of public service. The Labour candidate was Harold Lawrence to whom, since he was a pacifist, the Prime Minister, Clem Attlee (Major Attlee) refused to send the customary letter of commendation. Walter Monckton was a remarkable man, who understood ordinary people and had a great rapport with them, particularly with trade unionists, and his work as Minister of Labour in the Conservative Government was outstanding. Had he still been in office, he would never have allowed Ted Heath to get into his confrontation with the miners.

Previously in the 1949 local election, the Citizens had gained four seats from Labour, drawing level in the Council. Alderman Parish had commented 'the Tory machine was working at full pressure'. This showed great foresight because it was the Tory organisation of the postal vote in marginal seats which enabled them to win the 1951 General Election—despite Labour polling the largest number of votes that any party had ever received in a General Election.

Despite this organisation, there was no change in Bristol's 1951 General Election results. Ted Bishop, elected to the Council in 1946, fought Bristol West for Labour in 1950, Exeter in 1951 and South Gloucestershire in 1955 before being elected for Newark in 1964. Losing his seat in 1983, he was made a life peer and his premature death cut short the career of one of Labour's most loyal and conscientious servants.

A major re-distribution made both North West and North East much more marginal. In the General Election of 1955, Will Coldrick's majority was reduced to 876 and in Bristol North West, Sir Gurney Braithwaite was beaten by Labour's Chris Boyd, who although a thoroughly decent man, never seemed to be able to establish any real understanding, or rapport, with his activists, or the electorate, and it came as no surprise when he lost the seat in 1959 to Martin McLaren. Martin quickly established himself as a most popular and conscientious M.P. and held on in 1964 against Labour's David Watkins, a former city councillor and latterly M.P. for Consett in County Durham.

The Conservative candidate in Bristol South East in 1951 was Robin Cooke, soon to feature in a Bristol West by-election. When Sir Walter Monckton was returned in 1955 against the Labour candidate, Walter Johnson, his opponent told him he spoke more like a Labour man, to which Monckton replied 'the last person who said that to me was Clement Attlee'.

In March 1957 there was a by-election in Bristol West caused by Walter Monckton's elevation to the peerage. The favourite for the Conservatives was Kenelm Dalby, who had fought Bristol Central in 1951 and 1955, and was a pillar for the Conservatives on the City Council. George McWatters was also on the short list. He had been a city councillor and fought Bristol South in 1955, and later in 1959, and became a most successful businessman. Both were surprisingly beaten for the nomination by Robin Cooke. Robin Cooke's father was a very brilliant surgeon, and the unkind gossip at the time was that there were so many ladies at the selection conference who had either been under his knife, or were afraid they might have to be operated on, that personal fears over-rode political judgement. The Labour candidate was W. T. Rodgers, then General-Secretary of the Fabian Society, and later member for Stockton-on-Tees, Cabinet Minister and one of the 'Gang of Four'. I was present when he was selected and was one of only a handful of people to vote against his selection. I like to think it was foresight in view of his subsequent career, but in fact, I was wholly unimpressed by his slick presentation and apparent careerism. Nevertheless, there was a substantial swing to Labour in the bye-election, although Robin Cooke was returned with a majority of 14,162 to become the youngest M.P. As it turned out, Robin never really settled in the House of Commons and only found his niche after he had retired in 1983, when he became an adviser on the Refurbishment and Amenities of the Palace of Westminster. In this he excelled and his tragic early death robbed the House of a great and caring servant.

On the Council, Labour's fortunes were being eroded. During the May election in 1959, I canvassed for Jesse Stephen, a Labour and Co-operative stalwart, who had lost her seat the previous year and was attempting a come back in the Hillfields Ward. Jesse came from Clydeside and from her early years had organised women workers. I did not like the canvass results I obtained and reported this to Will Coldrick, the local M.P. He replied 'I will have to get cracking or I shall lose my seat'. Unfortunately, not only did Jesse fail to make a comeback, but Will Coldrick lost in the 1959 General Election to Alan Hopkins.

The losses in the May elections for Labour amounted to nine seats, including a colossal 30% swing against Labour in Easton, where Bill Cozens lost to an Eastern Home Defence Candidate. Reg Cunningham was beaten at Henbury by a ratepayer candidate and Ted Bishop lost at Brislington. Bob Wall, later to become Sir Robert Wall, beat Charles Merrett at Horfield: both were to become Leaders of the Council in the future.

The disastrous results for Labour had two main causes locally, apart from the national feeling of 'You have never had it so good' generated by Harold MacMillan, leading to his victory in the 1959 General Election. Labour had two large traditional reservoirs of support. First, on the council estates, but these were alienated by substantial rent increases. The other traditional area of support was the inner city areas of terraced houses. Here people were frightened to death by the nonsense that owners of unfit houses could only be offered a pound site value for their properties. In the Labour Party, some of us complained bitterly about this, to be told that this pitifully low compensation was laid down by an Act of Parliament and that if the City Council did not implement the law, then the Government would step in and do it for the Council. 'If that is the case,' we said 'then refuse to do it, let the Government get on with it and people will see where the blame really lies.' Unfortunately this advice was not taken, with disastrous electoral results. I, myself, was accused by Jesse Stephen of advocating anarchy (this may come as a surprise to some of the new activists of Bristol South Labour Party).

The loss of two Parliamentary seats in the 1959 General Election completed Labour's discomfiture. The only footnote I would add is that I was the Labour Candidate in Bristol West and was very proud of achieving a 0.1 percent swing to Labour, reducing the Conservative majority to 20,117.

The damage done to Labour could not easily be repaired, and in the 1960 local elections, every ward was contested for the first time and the Citizens gained power for the first time since 1951. Jack Fisk was beaten by a Ratepayer at Henbury, but Enid St. John, a pillar of the Education Committee, kept her seat at Southmead. Cyril Langham lost by five votes at St. George East, Vivian Thomas, the Council's youngest member, lost and Labour Group Secretary, Bill Cozens, lost Easton to another Home Defence candidate. Graham Robertson, a future Council Leader, lost Brislington. Ken Brown, Tory stalwart, organised an Auster on polling day, flying over the city urging people to vote Citizen.

Local events to be noted. On Saturday April 23rd, 1960 Lord Luke formally opened the Ashton Court Estate, bought from the Smythes for £100,000 a triumph for the foresight and vision of the planning committee chairman, Ald. Harry Hennessey. Harry and Lord Luke both planted trees to commemorate the event. On Monday May 2nd there was a Farewell Social & Dance for Bill Waring, leaving his post as Joint Secretary of the Trades Council and Borough Labour Party. Bill was also a long serving councillor, specializing in Housing.

On April 8th the death occurred of Sir John Inskip. A tribute was paid to him by Ald. Arthur Parish, which I think sums up what I have been trying to say about the way the Council worked in the immediate post war period: 'although we found ourselves in opposing political parties, this did not prevent a bond of friendship based on mutual understanding and a desire to serve, which strengthened as the years went by'.

Conservative organisation was centred on Orchard Street first under James Smith and then W. McKenzie Bell. It was becoming increasingly efficient, rarely breaking cover apart from well organised and publicised public meetings, with national figures and carefully drafted handouts from association meetings and dinners. The safe seat of Bristol West was organised from 5, Westfield Park, under the guidance of Gladys Pamphlett, still alive and in her 90s. As I said before, postal voting was the Conservative speciality and sometimes Martin McLaren's majority was similar to the number of postal votes registered in Westbury Ward alone. Martin stuck by Bristol when he lost his seat in 1966 and made a comeback in 1970. I think his political philosophy is hard to better when he said 'win without boasting, lose without complaining'.

Labour's organisation was centred on the Borough Labour Party at Kingsley Hall Old Market. Bill Waring was the secretary from 1949. Meetings were monthly and surprisingly in these days of paranoia against the press, reporters were admitted. The May Day rally and march were carefully organised and a large lorry always drove at the back of the Labour procession, the Communist Party had to follow behind this, so that there was a clear separation and no confusion in the spectators' minds. Unfortunately, this practice no longer occurs, and out of loyalty to my colleagues, I will refrain from any further comment. There were a number of full time constituency agents including the redoubtable Jack Knight, who was shared between Bristol Central and West, and was a notable Chairman of the Watch Committee, and Les Bridges in Bristol South, who later became secretary of the Borough Party and Trades Council.

The Co-operative Movement was always strong and produced a number of Council stalwarts, including Mrs. Tambling, Mrs. Heard, Mrs. Dare, Arthur Maddison and Roy Morris.

The Labour Party maintained a strong presence, although *Evening Post* editorials were constantly castigating the electorate after local elections for their lack of interest, referring in 1957 to 'appalling apathy'. The same point was made in June when Earl Attlee spoke in Bristol, when he warned that 'lack of interest might decay our democracy'. Nevertheless, if one looks at this reasonably objectively, Bristol was well run, whichever party was in power. The tragedy is that Bristol was carved up by local government re-organisation, and one notes that as far back as 1947 the City Council, commenting on proposed local government re-organisation, resolved 'that the present single-tier system of local Government for the City and County of Bristol is the simplest, and most efficient and economical for this area and should be retained'.

Party feelings ran deep over the Suez crisis in 1956. Public meetings called by Labour at short notice were packed out. Speakers included John Strachey. I often felt that Bristol's revolutionary fervour had burned itself out in the last century, and that Bristolians preferred the slow, steady progress. Over recent years there has been an influx of the hard left in Bristol, whether by accident or design, and in my view this has led to a weakening of Labour's appeal. In the mid 1950s Joe Holland moved to Bristol, having been selected as the Labour candidate for South Gloucestershire and formed a branch of Victory for Socialism, a left wing pressure group. I, myself, was a member for a time, but it never really got off the ground and was a cause of resentment amongst many traditional party members.

Unlike today, politics during this period was associated with fun and fellowship. People were very serious in their aims, drawing on their respective experiences, but the objectives of improving the well-being of Bristolians and the standing of the city, were the same, although obviously ideas differed as to how this should be done. Elections were also much more enjoyable and the percentage polls in local elections, when 43% was described and deplored as apathetic, would now be hailed as triumphs of electoral awareness, when party chiefs are pleased with polls of 30% and above.

General Elections were serious but had their humorous side. Mrs. Hall, a prominent Bristol West Conservative, used to parade up and down Whiteladies Road wearing sandwich boards during the Labour Government, proclaiming 'no beer, no stout, you put them in, you put them out'.

Councillor Roy Wilmott's deeds of sabotage of the Conservative machine in Bristol South are still talked of in awed tones by the old timers. All together, a good time for Bristol, when people of goodwill had a strong commitment to the city which often overcame political differences.

Show Biz in the Fifties

A trip down memory lane with Alston Thomas

Few in the arts or entertainment industry had a sharper wit or a more caustic tongue than the irascible Sir Thomas Beecham.

And that is something for which generations of Bristolians will always be grateful. For it was almost entirely due to the ridicule and scorn which the great conductor heaped on the City Council of the day that we have the present splendid Colston Hall.

The old hall, not for the first time, had gone up in flames early one Monday morning in 1945. The night before Carroll Gibbons and his Savoy Orpheans had made one of their rare trips away from London's Savoy Hotel to appear at one of Charles Lockier's famous Sunday Pops concerts. A carelessly discarded cigarette did the rest and Bristol had lost its fine hall for six years.

Eventually the City Council produced plans for a new hall, a modest one—or 'a single-storey glorified shed' as Sir Thomas was to scathingly dismiss it later.

In fairness to the Council, they felt it was the best they could probably manage. A Labour government obsessed with building council houses would not even give Bristol the steel to re-build its bomb-ravaged shopping centre so was unlikely to look kindly on a new concert hall.

Beecham was 70 in March 1949 and set off on a celebration tour with his Royal Philharmonic Orchestra, taking in Bath and Bristol. At the end of his concert in the Forum Cinema, Bath—itself not the West's greatest concert hall—he suddenly launched into a fierce attack on 'your barmy neighbours in Bristol'.

They promised to make themselves the laughing stock of the nation with their proposed new Colston Hall, he said. Bath loved it all, the Bristol press was appalled, some City Fathers apoplectic.

A few days later Beecham and his 'band' were due at the Central Hall, Old Market—the week-days substitute for the Colston Hall—and there was a sudden last minute rush for the few remaining tickets.

Not, it must be confessed, by music lovers, but those anxious to hear the second chapter of the Beecham saga. I was despatched to join them, to report the Maestro's speech and not to comment on his conducting.

As the *Evening Post* reported next day: 'There was an air of excited anticipation as the programme came to a close, with the majority of the capacity audience remaining in their seats in the hope that the celebrated conductor would "let fly" once more.

'For a time it looked as if they would be disappointed, but after they had clamoured for nearly ten minutes, Sir Thomas reappeared and amid deafening applause brought his guns to bear on the City Fathers once more.'

Explaining his previous outburst he said: 'I endeavoured to point out to you directly and them (the Corporation) indirectly that they were on the verge of making complete jackasses of themselves in the eyes of the whole world.'

He dismissed the shortage of steel excuses. London, he said, was about to have the £2 million Royal Festival Hall and a National Theatre costing 'one or two million—it doesn't matter which'—when it already had 50 theatres. Why then should Bristol be satisfied with 'this tiny building' seating barely 1,000? It was a 'highly comical outrage'.

Why indeed, Bristol agreed. Up to then most had felt that even a tiny hall was better than none. Suddenly the tide had changed. There were demands for a hall worthy of the city and these were met two years later when the hall, largely as it now is, was opened as part of the 1951 Festival of Britain celebrations. It was designed for use as a dance hall as well as a concert venue—that is why the front stalls are on the level. But I remember only one dance ever there, poorly attended and featuring, ironically, a band also from the Savoy Hotel.

Beecham died ten years later and I don't remember him ever appearing in what he was to claim 'my hall'.

But many of the other great conductors did, along with international orchestras, particularly from Eastern Europe booked by the mercurial Charles Lockier.

Working from a tiny office opposite the University he battled nobly while the hall was out of use. He used the Central Hall most nights for concerts ranging from symphony orchestras to a one-man recital by the harmonica king Larry Adler. Ted Heath and his orchestra made their first Bristol appearance in this hall.

On Sundays, the Central Hall, built as a Methodist Church, reverted to that use and Mr Lockier usually borrowed the giant Embassy Cinema. Its shallow stage was a handicap but Lockier managed to put sizeable dance bands, like Harry Roy's, on it. But the biggest money-spinners were the first appearances of the Ink Spots and the Sid Phillips Band.

But there was little official thanks to him for keeping the concert flag flying in those difficult years and when the Colston Hall was ready the Corporation's entertainments department played a bigger role, grabbed many of the stars and Mr Lockier found himself squeezed out. Under the Corporation there was heavy emphasis on weekly all-in wrestling, a huge money maker, and of course top-selling pop and rock stars.

These were trotted out almost weekly—sometimes with even greater frequency. Bobby Darin, Clyde McPatter, Emile Ford and Duane Eddy all

The ruined interior of the Colston Hall destroyed by fire in 1945.

appeared on the same bill, with Darin, surprisingly getting a very restive reception.

Acts picked to stand between Buddy Holly and his fans also had a roughish night.

A teenage Paul Anka, through no fault of his own, ushered in a new and unwelcomed phenomenon: girls, 4,000 of them, who screamed their way through his entire performances.

There were the giants of jazz, too, Armstrong, Teagarden, Bechet and Hines. Teagarden proved too much for one of my *Evening Post* colleagues. As we made our way back to the office he grabbed my arm, 'I've seen Jack Teagarden' he gasped—and burst into tears.

But one of the most significant nights was when Stan Kenton brought his band to town. Because of musician union disputes no American band had appeared in the city for 20 years. Most local band-leaders cancelled their engagements that night and fans travelled up to 80 miles.

Kenton was to have visited the F. W. Allen record shop to autograph records but promoter Lockier objected—'I don't want a tired bandleader on my hands' he protested. So Kenton sent his band off to their next gig in Cardiff, stayed overnight in Bristol and went to the shop next day. He also threw a party in the Royal Hotel for 150 record dealers, a gesture which delighted everyone. Except, perhaps, Mr Lockier.

While Bristol battled to get its fire-damaged Colston Hall rebuilt worse was to come. For in the lunch-hour of February 19th, 1948 fire swept through the stage of the Bristol Hippodrome. The entire backstage area was gutted, but miraculously firemen managed to prevent the flames spreading to the auditorium, although the fire safety curtain had not been lowered.

It was at the height of the pantomime season—*Babes in the Wood*, starring Old Mother Riley and 'her' daughter Kitty, Arthur Lucan and his quite awful wife, Kitty McShane.

She has been the subject of several TV documentaries since her death and those who saw her on the day of the fire would vouch that most of the unflattering things said about her were justified. She seemed little concerned about the loss of the theatre or the plight of her fellow artists suddenly without work. She ranted about the loss of Arthur's fine 'dame' costumes and nothing else seemed to matter.

'. . . the theatre, what about our costumes?' she raged.

At first Stoll Theatres had little more success in pleading with the government for materials to re-build the theatre than Bristol Corporation was having over the Colston Hall.

But astonishingly, by September they had got their building licence, set to work immediately and announced they would be back in business with a pantomime before the end of the year. And sure enough on Christmas Eve the curtain went up on *Cinderella* with Ted Ray as Buttons.

Lavish musicals followed in the succeeding months, *White Horse Inn, Lilac Domino* with a youthful Ian Carmichael, and a couple of Ivor Novello classics, *Glamorous Nights* and *King's Rhapsody* in which he had been starring when he died a few months earlier. Debonair Jack Buchanan replaced him.

Guys and Dolls got its European debut with Sam Levene, Stubby Kaye and the glamorous Vivienne Blaine there in May 1953 and there were other Broadway masterpieces, *The King and I, Carousel, Brigadoon, Annie Get Your Gun* and *South Pacific.*

In 1950 there were fewer than 150 TV sets in the city—the early ones got their pictures from the Midlands—and the television boom did not really get under way until the Coronation in 1953. So the great star-maker was the gramophone record and those who made the best-selling ones were to dominate most of the 50s.

Top pop singers took over the Hippodrome for weeks on end, most of them British while the Colston Hall entertained Americans, stars like Guy Mitchell and Frankie Laine.

Donald Peers, the hottest singing property of his day, came in 1950 and broke box office records that had stood for years. He was a sensation. The record stood until young Tommy Steele came.

Some careers began in the Hippodrome, others, sadly ended there.

Ruby Murray had five records in the Top 20 at the same time—no one else has ever achieved this. These, and TV appearances, had shot her to fame and she decided to branch into variety, starting at the Hippodrome. She was lucky to have acts like Morecambe and Wise, Harry Worth and Jimmy Wheeler in support.

Billy Eckstine, the American singing star, on the other hand had what the *Evening Post* called 'unambitious support' while the comedian Al Read closed the 1955 variety season backed 'by great slabs of mediocrity'.

Rose 'Chee Chee' Murphy, the singing pianist, launched her British career at the Hippodrome and the theatre figured early in the careers of Denis Lotis, Yana, Lita Rosa, Dickie Valentine and Ronnie Hilton, all big at the time.

But the Hippodrome also saw the final performance of the rock star Eddie Cochran, killed in Chippenham in April 1960 on his way from the theatre to Heathrow.

One of the most astonishing acts was that of the American 'mentalist' Harry Kahne, who wrote poetry on a blackboard, backwards, upside down, sideways, upwards and downwards and did complicated mathematical problems while all the time reciting Kipling. It was a remarkable piece of concentration which alas proved too much for the unique Mr Kahne. He died from a brain haemorrhage soon after leaving Bristol.

Less tragic was the farewell of Bristol's own Randolph Sutton who, with his 70th birthday coming up, announced his retirement at the Hippodrome, 66 years after his public debut standing on a chair in a church hall at the foot of Blackboy Hill. He went out in style with a bill which included Morecambe and Wise, the Bristol comedy impressionists Tony Fayne and David Evans, Eve Boswell and two great Welsh favourites, Gladys Morgan and Ossie Morris.

After interminable weeks of recording stars the Hippodrome decided on a season of comics, launched by the tragic Tony Hancock, whose parents incidentally were Bristolians.

The omens could not have been less promising for the doubt-tortured

Hancock. There was the first match of the new football season, a top-selling recording star close by in the Colston Hall and a luxury cinema was being re-opened in the city. More morose than ever he would don his black Homburg hat and retire to a dark corner backstage trying to gauge the mood of his unseen audience and plucking up courage to face them.

His opening night could have been disastrous. One of his acts called for him to throw a tennis ball in vexation at an unseen figure off-stage, who would retaliate by bombarding 'Ancock with scores of tennis balls.

Unfortunately the 'assistant' allowed himself to be detained overlong at the Bunch of Grapes on the other side of Denmark Street.

Tony despatched his missile, but nothing came back, until stage hands with great presence of mind took over pelting Hancock with hastily-gathered balls. Normally, Hancock could have been expected to disintegrate under such an experience, but he apparently much enjoyed the set-back.

Astonishingly, much the same thing happened the following week when Harry Secombe brought his *Rocking the Town* show in which he had starred at the London Palladium for nine months. Among the hand-picked members of the George Mitchell Singers chosen as his 'backing group' was the late Tony Mercer, later to become tremendously popular in the Black and White Minstrels' TV series.

He, too, lingered in the Grapes too long. Secombe, normally much more tolerant and easy going than Hancock, was on this occasion not best pleased with a very contrite Mr Mercer.

Almost as insecure as Hancock was the trumpet star Eddie Calvert, who later died in South Africa. Each night he would drink a bottle of rum before he could face his audience. On his opening night in Bristol his road manager, worried about the drinking, had, he thought, a brilliant idea. The Bunch of Grapes, he told Eddie, only sold half-bottles. 'That's all right' said Calvert. 'Fetch a second one'.

Comedians were usually good value. Max Miller came every year, his popularity undiminished. Norman Evans, one of the greatest pantomime dames ever, was discovered in a Hippodrome panto. Ted Ray made his panto debut also running a competition to name his first radio series (he chose *Ray's a Laugh*).

But the biggest welcome was owed Jimmy James, one of the best stage 'drunks', not only for some marvellous comedy routines, but also for the fact that there was a theatre left. He had been on the bill in 1941 when incendiary bombs rained down. He had volunteered for fire-watching duty on the roof and kicked every bomb into the street below before they could do much damage.

Radio was still 'king' and the theatre usually had to wait for the top series to be rested before seeing the stars. These included Arthur English, Max Wall, Benny Hill—who made his early broadcasts from Bristol—Peter Sellers, Michael Bentine, Jewell and Wariss, and singing attractions, the Radio Revellers and the Five Smith Brothers.

Not all the big American names made a lot of money—at least not for the theatre. Tyrone Power came in Shaw's *Devil's Disciple* playing to rows of empty seats. A week later Lloyd Nolan starred in a superb production of the

Sir Thomas Beecham whose ridicule of the city fathers forced Bristol to rebuild the Colston Hall on a fitting scale.

Tony Hancock, the unhappy genius, avoided a disastrous first night at Bristol Hippodrome.

Cain Mutiny Court Martial, again to vast vacant spaces.

But the biggest disappointment, in the light of his later mega-success was Frank Sinatra. He came in 1953 and you could have bought seats by the row. The Fleet Street press was giving him a hard time, principally because of his association with Ava Gardner, but he was extremely charming in his dealing with the Bristol newspapers.

Al Martino was enormously popular when he came—and was to become even more so later. But his week in Bristol had its setbacks. The orchestra was augmented to 24 and were crammed into the pit instead of on stage as he was accustomed to in America.

There were times when he could barely be heard, but he pointed out the orchestra would have had to be paid 25 per cent more to play behind him on stage, as Billy Ternent's had for Sinatra.

The 'real gone gall' Nellie Lutcher, a sepia songstress with several hit records got an extremely cordial welcome, but never threatened box office records.

Two more Hollywood stars, Chico Marx and the lugubrious Mischa Auer both played the piano, rather well, but neither drew the crowds.

A *Western Daily Press* critic, later a top BBC official, panned Marx—forgetting the star was to judge his paper's prestigious Kingswood Carnival Queen competition later in the week. That took a lot of sorting out.

There was ballet occasionally, and the Carl Rosa Opera Co was still going strong—how we loved Bristolians talking about the Carl Rosal Operal Co. It was the company that brought to Bristol the Maltese tenor Oreste Kirkop, who was then being hailed as a world-beater and was to enjoy some Hollywood success although not all that had been predicted.

The late Mario Lanza also spent a week there, a constant menace to any woman foolish enough to enter his dressing room!

But the most consistently popular was of course the D'Oyly Carte with their Gilbert and Sullivan operas. Houses were sold out weeks in advance and there was an outcry when the annual season was reduced from three weeks to a fortnight.

But one year they came unstuck when they included Holy Week in their season. Ticket sales plummeted. Strange to reflect that not many years later supermarkets were opening on Good Friday and the D'Oyly Carte was no more.

The year 1948 was in many ways a depressing one for Bristol, with both the Colston Hall and the Hippodrome closed by fire. But at that marvellous little institution, the Little Theatre, an undamaged part of the Colston Hall, there were celebrations. It had been 25 years since its opening by Rupert Harvey.

In those years 802 different plays had been presented, 50 of them receiving their world premiere—by the time it closed in 1962 the figure had risen to more than 70. For much of the time they put on a different play every week before eventually going in for fortnightly seasons.

Many who became famous in films and in the West End had their careers launched at the Little, Mervyn Johns, Geoffrey Keen, Terence de Marney, Sebastian Shaw, Barry Sinclair, Cyril Luckham and Richard Goolden among them.

Ronald Russell and Peggy Ann Wood always managed to assemble teams that attracted enormous affection: Paul Lorraine, not the best memory on stage but a marvellous talent for making up lines as he went along, Travers Cousins, Malcolm Farquhar, Connie Chapman, Ruth Porcher who was to die tragically young, Jane Comfort and Lockwood West come immediately to mind.

It was all done against a background of financial strain. The year the company made a profit of £3 was cause for celebration. Astonishingly, when the curtain came down finally the theatre was losing only £1,000 a year, less than it was paying in rent and rates to its landlord, Bristol Corporation, who many felt could have done a lot more to help the much-loved Rapier Players.

The Empire Theatre—or the New Empire as it became in 1954—was a much-maligned place. It is remembered almost exclusively for its lovely pantomimes, and a whole string of so-called nude shows where unclothed ladies posed motionless, usually recreating some great master painting. The Lord Chamberlain banned any sort of movement by the girls who decorated the stage week after week. There were two notable star nudes, Phyllis Dixey who retired to Pill, and a succession of Janes of the *Daily Mirror*.

The titles of the weekly revues were usually more provocative than the entertainment, *Naughty Nudes of 1948*, *Date With Eve*, *Naughty, Nutty and Nice*, *Strike a Nude Note*, *Fanny Get Your Fun* and *Strip Strip Hooray*, which turned out to be one of the best-dressed shows ever at the theatre.

But the theatre's owner, a Bournemouth hotelier, F J Butterworth, was frequently on the lookout for something different. When the Little Theatre closed for a while he put in the Harry Hanson Players, with a great reputation on the South Coast.

They were a good deal better than most of the company at the Little and gave Bristol a rare chance of seeing the works of Tennessee Williams and Jean Paul Sartre, but the traditional Little patron was unprepared for the

Respectable Prostitute, Men Without Shadows with its realistic torture scenes, or razor-slashing dramas.

FJB even tried a novel mixture of drama and variety, a gangster play set in a night club which gave an opportunity to feature cabaret acts in the club. It starred Cy Grant.

Bands and musical acts were always in demand, Big Bill Campbell and his 'cowboy' singers, Troise and his Banjoliers, Macari and his Dutch Serenaders (all Macari's children who later became famous with other bands were born in Bristol), the Dagenham Girl Pipers, Harry Roy, the Radio Revellers, Sid Millward and his Nitwits and Syd Seymour and His Mad Hatters.

All the FJB courage and optimism came to an end in August 1954. More than 170 young hopefuls turned up on the Sunday to audition for Carol Levis and his latest *Stairway to Success* discoveries at the theatre.

Most were rejected within a minute or two. Those selected rarely got more than one or two rungs up the Levis ladder and at the end of the week, after 60 years, the Empire had closed for the last time.

Bravely the manager, Roddy Annat, told the packed house: 'It is appropriate that the last performances should be given by a company of "discoveries". You have seen this stage peopled with the stars of the past, stars of the present, and now stars of the future.'

Bristol Corporation bought the theatre for under £35,000, let it to the BBC for a few years and then knocked it down to make way for the Old Market underpass, and eventually the Holiday Inn.

Although business boomed in the Bristol theatres and the Colston Hall, the city's main entertainments were the cinemas and dance halls. At the outbreak of war Bristol had built 60 cinemas and at one time 42 were still in use.

But by the mid-1950s, the supermarket boom was under way and cinemas, now beginning to lose their patrons to television, made a ready home for them.

Announcing in September 1956 that the little Brislington cinema was up for sale after 40 years, the *Evening Post* pointed out that its closure 'brings the number of cinemas in the city, once 42, down to 27.' Cinemas were still paying a heavy entertainments tax then, and this was blamed for the loss of several of them.

One of the most reluctant cinemas to die was the tiny News Theatre, one of the few survivors of air-raids on the Wine Street-Castle Street shopping centre. Four of the demolition workers were hurt when they crashed to the ground as a floor collapsed, and there were other accidents.

There was also a row following allegations that a coloured workman—and there were not many of those around in 1959—was being paid less than the white.

One of the most unexpected closures was the lovely Cabot at Filton. Sidney Gamlin, a member of Bristol City Council, owned it and spent £4,000 on modernising it to meet the competition of TV. He got a lot of it back through showing *South Pacific* week after week. But after a year he had sold out to a supermarket.

The closure of his other cinema, the much-loved Park in St George, was a more bizarre affair. He learned that two of its staff were having an affair, although one at least was married. A fiery, but well-meaning, little man of high moral principles, he sacked both. The rest of the staff protested. He was unimpressed. The cinema closed overnight, never again to open.

Dancing was hugely popular with the top venues being the Victoria Rooms and the ballroom of the Grand Spa Hotel, Clifton.

'See you at the Vic tonight' was a regular promise and there could still be found the 'big bands' of Ken Lewis, Lew Barclay and Ralph Bright. Ken eventually became a full-time official of the Musicians Union, Lew went into promoting Ideal Homes exhibitions, and Ralph landed long-term contracts outside the city. An era ended with them.

The Grand Spa sparked countless romances as couples danced between splendid marble pillars to fine bands booked by Reginald Williams, who had had his own top band in the 1930s at the Coliseum in Park Row. He was the first to employ the brilliant international pianist George Shearing in a recording studio.

Reg Williams also developed a cabaret policy at the Grand Spa, featuring many youngsters destined to be stars: Shirley Bassey, Petula Clark, Peter Sellers, Benny Hill and many others.

Outside competition came when the band-leader and former journalist, Eric Winstone, took over the giant Bristol South Baths when it closed for the winter. His band played there sometimes and he also put in others, like Jerry Allen's. But after three years it all went sour, with fights and riots in the hall, culminating in smoke bombs being thrown. Mr Winstone alleged 'organised sabotage'.

By then Mecca, the biggest dance hall owners, had bought the little ballrooms in an old quarry at The Glen on Durdham Down. Top bands, Harry Roy's and Ray Ellington's were resident, and then the company built a new ballroom, the Locarno in the quarry. It opened with Geraldo there for a week and then Ambrose for another, and was extremely popular, but eventually Mecca built even bigger dance halls in the New Bristol Centre, close to the Colston Hall and the Glen, too, was no more.

The great newspaper war of the 1930s, following the launch of the *Evening Post* in 1932, had been over for 10 years when the 'other' war ended in 1945. But the *Evening Post* and the *Evening World* still had their problems for newsprint was to be rationed for another 10 years, stifling some of the commercial competition between them. Editorial rivalry never diminished with reporters from both papers striving every day to put one over on the competition. Because of paper and petrol rationing and other distribution problems the *Post* and the *World* had territorial agreements. Both competed for readers in Bristol and Weston-super-Mare, but the *World* was allocated Taunton and Bridgwater while the *Post* dominated Yeovil and South Somerset to an astonishing degree—at one time the *Post* had sales of 8,000 a day in the Yeovil area when the town's population was only 22,000. Penetration of that kind in Bristol would have made it a fortune.

But by the early 1950s, a new circulation battle was on with the *Post* opening offices in Gloucestershire, Chippenham and other areas new to it.

Rent or buy
we look after it!

FREE service, **FREE** tubes, valves, etc., **continuously** IF YOU RENT, for 2 years IF YOU BUY

IF YOU RENT

Continuous **FREE** service, tubes, valves, etc. Rentals reduce every 6 months.

TELEVISION from **9/-** per week
RADIOGRAM from **3/-** per week
RADIO from **1/10** per week

IF YOU BUY

2 years' **FREE** service, 2 years' **FREE** tubes, 2 years' **FREE** valves, etc.

14" Table, Multi-Channel T.V.
     Cash Price **65** gns.

17" Table, Multi-Channel T.V.
     Cash Price **74** gns.

17" Console, Multi-Channel T.V.
     Cash Price **86** gns.

HIRE PURCHASE terms available

RADIO RENTALS LTD

FREE!
36-PAGE
COLOUR
BOOK

--COUPON--
711

(World's largest Radio and T.V. Service Organisation)

29, ST. STEPHEN'S STREET, BRISTOL 1.   Tel. 2-4397
220, CHELTENHAM ROAD BRISTOL 6.   Tel. 4-5007
194, STAPLETON ROAD, BRISTOL 5.   Tel. 5-6524
104, MIDDLE STREET, YEOVIL.   Tel. 2403

Please send me FREE 36-page BOOK giving full details of Renting and Buying with FREE Service

Name ....

Address ....

No stamp needed if posted

The 1950s saw television emerge as the great popular entertainer. All sets were black and white in those days. By the mid 1950s, the effect on cinema audiences was gathering pace and Bristol cinemas, once numbering 42, were down to 27.

Then, in 1959, came a disastrous nationwide strike of printers which saw all three Bristol newspapers suspended.

On July 2nd, the first edition of a brand new paper, *News of the West*, hit the Bristol streets.

A notice across the top of the front page explained: 'At another crisis point in Bristol's newspaper history 27 years ago, there appeared a newspaper under the brilliant editorship of Richard Hatt. It was called *The Bristol Paper.* Some may have forgotten, but not those Bristol journalists for whom it was a lifeline, guiding them to the start of a new life of service to the public. It was not intended to do more than to serve readers in a period when they were denied two newspapers which were dear and trusted friends.

'Today we introduce another such newspaper. Its editor is anonymous, its staff volunteers, its purpose the same as Hatt's paper, to serve readers and advertisers while Bristol is denied its regular daily reading. It will also safeguard the future livelihood of the men and women caught up in the present dispute.'

It was a much-praised newspaper, but sadly its hopes of safeguarding 'the future livelihood of the men and women caught up in the dispute' were not to be.

For the strike proved fatally damaging. Inside a year the much-loved *Western Daily Press* had lost its independence and its Baldwin Street home, becoming instead part of the *Evening Post* group.

A worse fate was to be suffered by the *World*. In February 1962 it became the 16th national or provincial daily paper to close in nine years and many of its splendid reporters, including those who got *News of The West* going, were out of work.

In the late 1940s the *Post* had a daily circulation of 120,000 with the *World* not that far behind with 90,000.

But by the time the *World* closed it was reckoned to be selling not many more than 30,000 compared with the *Post's* 196,000.

Official *Western Daily Press* circulation figures were hard to come by, but were understood to be a mere 12,000 on weekdays—ruinously low for a daily paper—rising to 28,000 on Saturdays when the auctioneers and estate agents advertisements were printed.

Under the *Evening Post* umbrella, though, its sales rocketed to more than 80,000 a morning and have remained fairly consistent ever since.

By then both the *Post* and the *Press* were under the intense competition of television and later local radio. Bristol had to share its TV service with, and receive its pictures from Wales, even after TWW, the original commercial programme, had opened its own studios in Brislington in 1960.

Sporting Types

David Foot looks back on local heroes of the
Fifties

There are, when it comes to sport, so many Saturdays to cherish—so many
peaks and moments of elation, so many heroes in red or blue-and-white
quartered shirts. We think of Atyeo's arrival and Hammond's sad departure.
We think of cavalier, revolutionary rugby at the Memorial Ground. The
memory is romantically selective. So we can forget (more or less) the
boardroom conflicts and the alleged temperamental flaws which are
supposed to leave a West Country sportsman deficient when it comes to steel
and fibre.

I'd long been seduced by the cigarette-card glamour of professional sport.
Now I had arrived in Bristol, joyfully with a wife-to-be on my arm and an
unbridled affection for cricket and, only slightly less so, for rugby and
soccer, passionately described to me by a bright-eyed pre-war Somerset
socialist as 'theatre of the working classes.'

Up to then, my cricket-watching had in the main been limited to
occasional Bank Holiday visits on the single-track train to see my native
county play at Taunton. Football, by contrast, had been fervently witnessed
from a windswept position between the cow-pats on the touchline of my
village ground—or later, as a cub reporter, from the lofty extremity of a
rickety stand at Yeovil's Huish.

At Bristol, it was to be the county ground in Nevil Road, the Memorial
Ground, Ashton Gate and homely Eastville. I remember how I was still full
of tingling boyish enthusiasms, untainted by the reservations of cynicism that
came later with experience and perspective. The changing sports panorama,
coming as I did from the depths of the rural West Country, was a thrilling
prospect. Nevil Road was Lord's, Ashton Gate was White Hart Lane. Anne,
my imminent wife, was much more level-headed. For her the sporting scene
wasn't changing so drastically: she assumed she'd still be helping with the
Sunday cricket teas, still be expected to applaud me loyally when I moved
into double figures.

This can be no more than an impression, a flavour, of sport in Bristol
during the dozen or 15 years after the war. It was the period when grounds
were given an overdue lick of paint and crowds were returning in their

thousands, clasping at football, rugby and cricket as joyous therapy after all the misery, restriction and austerity.

For East Bristol, the marvellous climax came in 1952-53. Rovers, functional, warm-hearted, historically the poor relations, won promotion to the second division for the first time. There wasn't too much doubt about it: they went 27 games without defeat at one point. It was a triumph of native fervour and resolve. The Eastville dressing room in those days reverberated to the laughter and banter of accents as authentically Bristol as the old Frome which meandered past the ground.

Eastville itself had been controversially sold to the greyhound company for what looked to some like a relative pittance, in 1940. Criticism simmered on after the war when an official inquiry was held. Harsh words were spoken; the hapless Brough Fletcher, a manager who had demonstrated an undeniable aptitude for talent-spotting, found himself out of a job.

Into the vacant managerial office stepped Bert Tann, a Londoner few in Bristol had even heard of. But he came on the recommendation of the then FA secretary Stanley Rous. 'He's the young man to give you a lift—and he's a very good coach', said the elder statesman.

Tann had been a decidedly ordinary footballer with Charlton. His great skill was off the field. He was an intelligent man, with a pragmatic approach to tactics as they affected an unsophisticated West Country club. He was the best talker the club had ever known; he monopolised debate in the boardroom. The directors were rightly in awe of him. They were a sincere, introvert coterie—and that suited Bert.

There was an inhibiting No Buy-No Sell policy at the club, although just occasionally there were ways round it. Tann worked on what he had got: mostly local lads, with an endearing, old-fashioned pride in the team. Some of them, the manager quickly discovered, had exceptional talent. One, Geoff Bradford, played for England against Denmark in 1956.

Bradford had few frills. But he had two excellent feet, and an instinctive vision of the opposing goal. He was apt to turn centre halves into emotional wrecks. There were nine hat-tricks from him and 242 league goals. He came back from a broken leg to score goals and leave age-old terrace supporters with a glazed look of ecstasy, and tears unashamedly in the eyes. Geoff was a phlegmatic and lethal hero.

But the fans would have argued he was one of the many. The half-back line of Pitt, Warren and Sampson had the sound of a music hall act. Their names had the ring of absolute reliability . . . and much affection. The styles were contrasting and complementary. Behind them, Harry Bamford was probably the most loved of all!. Gentle, exasperating Harry. He was a defender of great natural skill, though he would persist in complicating life for himself within the penalty area. The modesty was as appealing as the standards of good behaviour he set for himself. He went on an FA tour to Australia; with a more fashionable club, he'd have walked into the England team. We all cried when he was killed in a motor cycle accident.

Where do we stop? Promoted Rovers weren't bogged down by soccer theory. It's said the first time Bert Tann, as a concession to changing trends, felt duty-bound to try out a 4-2-4 formation, the team were disastrously

*Left: Wally Hammond
leads the Gloucestershire
team off the field.*

*The master batsman in
action.*

beaten: and he encouraged the players to start playing by instinct again. So many names to remember. Fox and Watling (the latter who dispensed the jokes and professed to play the piano on away trips), Petherbridge and Lambden, Hoyle and Roost. And the others, most of them characters, surrounded by Eastville folk-lore and apocryphal tales.

Rovers were to stay in the second division for nine years. They once came very near climbing into the first. The next batch of names included Biggs and Jarman, Sykes and Hooper. Tann was moving sideways to take over as general manager, making way for another engaging Londoner, Fred Ford.

For Bristol City, promotion came in the 1954-55 season. Up to then, they had simply kept banging the goals in excitingly. A former rugby centre and footballing wing half had set the pattern. Don Clark was a Bristol boy who possessed rare co-ordination. He actually scored 42 goals in league and cup one season, and only injury put an end, in effect, to his prodigious feats.

By the promotion year John Atyeo had taken over. He had the perfect physique and most of the attributes of the perfect centre forward. His father was his mentor and negotiated with Harry Dolman before the young forward chose City in preference to Portsmouth. Atyeo was an intelligent Wiltshireman who preferred to play as a part-timer. At first he trained as a quantity surveyor, later as a schoolmaster.

His achievements are indelibly engrained on the memory, as where those years before of Billy Wedlock. Atyeo played six times for England—and netted five times for his country, a splendid ratio which might have been more generously recognised with additional appearances. He scored 314 goals for City in the league alone, 349 if you include the cup matches. His behaviour record was impeccable; he carried on a cordial never fractious, relationship with a succession of referees.

Just like Rovers, City had players of loyal Bristol blood. There were Guy and Bailey at full back, and Peacock just in front. If the loping, blond Guy was renowned for the length of his kicks, Peacock's fame emanated from a fiery temperament, only equalled by the measure of charm and innocence off the field. Dennis Roberts, who blocked the middle with unwavering efficiency, only looked a Bristolian; he actually came from Nottinghamshire. More authentically local were Cliff Morgan, Cyril Williams and Tony Cook.

Tommy Burden, with the Hampshire birth certificate, the Leeds United pedigree and the Glastonbury vowels, arrived to bolster the promotion challenge. So did Arthur Milton, once of Cotham Grammar School, who argued that there was a better long-term future for him in cricket. He stayed at Ashton Gate only until the end of the season and was apt to say, maybe tongue-in-cheek, that no-one asked him to come back for another year. Milton, Arsenal winger and Gloucestershire batsman, is assured of a place in the sporting history books as the last of the double internationals.

The boardroom would occasionally throb with discord. George Jenkins, the wing-collared chairman who as chairman had often been as chirpy and bright as the red carnation in his buttonhole, left in a rage after the annual meeting in 1949. He was asked to become a life member and he vehemently shook his head. Bob Hewison resigned at about the same time, resenting criticism of the way he chose the team. At various times there was

John Atyeo of Bristol City and England in 1957.

John Blake—advocate of the open style of rugby which made the Bristol club so exciting to watch.

BRISTOL EVENING POST

No. 5,028—1½d.   The Paper All Bristol Asked For and Helped to Create   Sat., July 3 1948

COOK'S BID FOR TEST HONOUR

Australian "Stars" Dismissed by Left-hander

The Men From Australia

BRILLIANT CENTURY BY MORRIS

Glo'shire Bowlers Face Formidable Task

(By JOHN COE)

MORRIS, in enterprising mood, took heavy toll of the bowling after Hassett, who led the Australians in place of Bradman, won the toss against Glo'shire at the County Ground, Bristol.

Cook, however, struck the first blow for Glo'shire, getting Barnes brilliantly caught in the slips by Crapp.

The Tetbury left-hander was again cheered when he lured Hassett out of his crease and Andy Wilson whipped off the bails in a trice.

A CENTURY BEFORE LUNCH

HUNDREDS were still pouring in when Lindsay Hassett and Basil Allen went out to examine the wicket.

The news that the Australians had won the toss and would bat raised the wildfire and the crowd settled down to a run point of a increasing easy wicket.

The previous record attendance for the ground was 17,500 Glo'shire v Somerset Aug 1946.

The umpires were Frank Lee, the former Somerset opening batsman and K McCanlis.

At 12.23 Allen led his men out to the accompaniment of a round of applause which was magnified a moment later when Morris and Barnes appeared to the wicket.

Barnett Opens

Barnett opened the attack from the pavilion end and his first delivery was pushed off his legs for a single past forward short-leg towards mid-wicket for a single by Barnes.

The first over was comparatively unproductive from a runs point of view and Colin Scott, bowling heavy fast followed with a maiden over to Barnett in his second.

Scott had three slips when he came on again. He worked up some pace and Andy Wilson kept peculiarly further back. But Barnes, taking advantage of a rather loose delivery for the first ball, hit it to the boundary for four.

Changed Ends

With seven on the board, Allen had the sense to switch Scott to leg and then booked Andy Wilson further up. This enabled Barnes to give illustration of his aggressive ability.

Barnett was unwise enough to send down a slightly under-pitched ball and away it was sent through the covers, with

THE SCORE

AUSTRALIANS.—First Innings.
S. Barnes, c Crapp, b Cook 44
A. Morris, not out 158
A. Hassett, st Wilson, b Cook 21
K. Miller, c Cook, b Scott . 51
R. Harvey, not out 8
Extras 5
___
Total (for 3 wickets) ..327

backward point trying vainly to intercept it.

A half-hearted appeal for l.b.w. against Barnes when he was in his early teens was treated by the crowd as a huge joke. Barnes, a stockily-built player, seemed to share their enjoyment.

Scott was quickly to learn that anything short of a length was fatal when Barnes was the batsman.

The Australian square-cut him beautifully and a forcing shot off the back foot was right out of the text-book.

After half an hour's play 30 runs were on the board, to which Barnes had contributed 27.

Keen Fielding

The score mounted steadily as Barnes glanced Scott to leg and then hooked him off his eyebrows to the long-leg boundary. The Glo'shire fielding was as keen as the occasion demanded. Andy Wilson, alert as ever, reached a ball that got up sharply by making an acrobatic spring. The Glo'shire bowling now came in for some heavy punishment.

Chief sufferer was Scott, who bowling erratically on the leg side, was hit again and again to the boundary rails.

A shout of anticipatory delight greeted the arrival of Tom Goddard at 51. Truth to tell, we half believed the veteran spinner might at least be able to tie the batsmen down, even if he did not actually claim a victim.

3 Boys in a Kiosk

A Bristol policeman on his rounds early this morning found three boys asleep in a telephone kiosk.

They had come from Gloucester to see the Glo'shire v Australia cricket match, and had sought this haven near the County Ground.

THE AUSTRALIAN TEAM, with Hamence as 12th man, who are playing against Glo'shire today, and the backgrounds Ashley Grange, where the great Dr W. G. Grace lived when he played for the county photographed by Mr H. A. Summers, of Kingsdown. Situated close to the County Ground, it was partly demolished some years before the war.

"M-AID WILL NOT CLOSE GAP"

Eden on Government "Spending Drag"

MR. Anthony Eden told his constituents at Warwick today that the heaviest drag on national effort was the high rate of Govt. expenditure.

"We are still spending at three times the rate before the war, and there is a growing conviction everywhere that we are not getting value for money.

"If we are still falling short of the supreme national effort required, the fault lies with the Govt. who hamper, confine, and distort our national economy," he said.

"The generous assistance we are to be given by the U.S. will certainly not cover the whole of the present gap.

"The most we can hope to receive this year is between £25 million and £30 million a month. On the latest information available the rate of expenditure of our reserves is still substantially above this.

"Taxation on enterprise and effort continue at rates which impose intolerable handicaps. British commercial greatness was built on raw-taking and cannot survive without it. Yet we have reached a position where it does not pay anyone to take risks.

"If he makes a profit Sir Stafford Cripps takes almost all of it. If he makes a loss he foots the bill himself. You cannot run a complex industrial and commercial nation indefinitely on that basis."

The Nat. Union of Railwaymen employees in Southampton Docks today decided not to impose their boycott on overtime. At an open air meeting 400 men were notified of the results of negotiations which took place yesterday between their representatives and railway executive officers. The proposals made by the latter were acceptable to the men.

BACK PAGE ✸

DRIVEN AWAY IN A LORRY

Gang's Whisky Haul in Bristol

Thieves who broke into a bonded warehouse at Canons' Marsh early today got away with a large quantity of whisky, believed to have been driven away in a lorry which they loaded on the premises.

THE theory is that the robbery was well planned, and that the lorry was backed into the doors of the warehouse to force the padlocks.

Having gained access the thieves selected the whisky and loaded it into their lorry.

Before driving off with their valuable haul, the thieves replaced the smashed padlocks with locks they brought with them, apparently to allay suspicions until they had made their getaway.

Employees discovered the premises had been entered when they arrived for work.

HOLIDAY RUSH

Extra Trains Stand By

Holiday traffic swept into a higher tempo today when there was a big increase in the number of people leaving the main London stations.

All trains at Temple Meads were well packed, and an official described the holiday rush as "beginning to make itself felt."

At Paddington indications were that today would probably be one of the busiest Saturdays this season. There were huge crowds for all the principal trains to the West. By 10 a.m. 10,220 passengers had left Paddington, compared with 4,841 at the same time last Saturday.

RATHER COOL

Bristol had 5.4 hours of sunshine yesterday, with a maximum temperature during the day of 63.7deg.

Forecast:

S.W. England: Moderate N. winds; mainly cloudy; bright periods in the East; mainly rather cool. Midday temperature 60-65 degrees.

Further Outlook: Continuing fair.

Lighting-up: Tonight, 10.29 p.m. to 3.58 a.m.; tomorrow, 10.29 p.m. to 3.59 a.m.

NEW DEVELOPMENT IN BALKAN BREAK-UP

Slav— Albania Split

Albania has denounced all existing economic agreements with Yugoslavia and has asked that all Yugoslav specialists leave Albania within 48 hours, the Yugoslavia News Agency said to-day.

ALBANIA decision to break off economic relations was contained in a Note handed to the Yugoslav Embassy in Tirana, the agency added.

The specialists told to leave include all technicians, professors, and other Yugoslav citizens sent to Albania to give brotherly aid for the country's reconstruction.

Announcing Albania's decision, the Agency published a communiqué stressing its ministerial character without previous consultations with the Yugoslav Govt, and "in contradiction to all fundamental principles of international law and of respect for international engagements."

Three Yugoslav protest Notes had been sent to the Albanian Foreign Office.

Note one protested against "provocative" incidents, including the tearing down of a portrait of Marshal Tito by an Albanian official in the offices of the jointly operated railway directorate in Tirana.

Note two protested against stoppage of work on the Yugoslav-Albanian railways project, cessation of oil and mining material, shipments from Albania to Yugoslavia, and a slow-down in the loading of Yugoslav ships.

This Note also demanded that the Albanian Govt. send to Belgrade without delay the Commission for settling differences between the two nations which was agreed upon earlier this year.

Note three protested against the dismissal of a Yugoslav political instructor attached to the Albanian Army who had been ordered to leave Albania immediately.

disapproval over the sale of Roy Bentley to Newcastle and Cyril Williams to West Brom.

As chairman, after Jenkins, came Harry Dolman. He had direct links with the club for 40 years, ending up as president. He could be autocratic and didn't always take kindly to fellow directors who had a conflicting point of view. His influence on the club-manifested by his boyish enthusiasm and undimmed optimism was considerable. He headed an engineering firm which he first joined as a junior draughtsman: that was the measure of his drive and resourcefulness. His skills as an inventor brought success to his firm. He designed the first floodlighting system for Ashton Gate. By present standards, the modest clumps of lights were unsophisticated. But he was still almost ahead of the field. Wolves came for the inaugural floodlit friendly and the match attracted a gate of 24,000. Dolman had seen the commercial value of evening games.

Harry was a man of persuasive charm. Yet it must be said that a high proportion of the theoretically corporate boardroom decisions, often enterprising ones, were his. He was an astute businessman—and usually had his own ideas about the kind of players and managers that the City needed.

Pat Beasley was one of his best appointments, even though this particular manager eventually went the inevitable way of the breed. He came in 1950 and was sacked early in 1958. Pat was unpretentious and laconic. He didn't go in for headline-catching imagery. But he had an impressive background as a player; he'd been a member of Arsenal's glamorous championship side of the Thirties and had earned an international cap against Scotland just before the war.

He was in charge when City won promotion to the second division. He encouraged his players to go for goal. His tactics were uncomplicated and effective. City were also bolstered in those days by large, loyal crowds. There were nearly 30,000 present to see Atyeo's debut (when he scored) and just as many to see Arsenal in what was only a friendly.

Before the Fifties had gone, Peter Doherty had arrived as the manager. The Irish genius still carried an aura of glamour. His stay was relatively short and unproductive. Maybe he expected too much from lesser mortals. Maybe he came up against an element of antipathy when it came to handling some of the experienced West Country players. Dressing room factions formed. It was a period of wariness and unease. City were on their way back to the third division. Peter Doherty, who could be delightful company and a word-spinner, was left shaking his head and clearing his desk.

Bristol Football Club (we have moved on to rugby) had quickly picked up the traces again after the war. Those were the days of Fred Hill and George Gibbs, the mobile prop who deserved his international recognition in 1947-48. Gibbs was captain for three seasons, Jack Gregory, the Olympics sprinter for two. And then came Bert Macdonald. A change was on the way; some put it more dramatically as a revolution.

Macdonald was a forward but he didn't believe blindly that the pack wins all the games for you. He began the talking and the reshaping. John Blake dared to put them into practice. Bristol became the most discussed club in the country. They achieved that reputation because they were different. They rediscovered the handling game; they turned it into an art form.

Blake had come out of the RAF. He was pale, clean-cut, intense. He was a perfect gentleman and believed that matches should be played in the open style of an exhilarating sixth-form contest. The boot was virtually forbidden. Those who kicked needlessly to touch were made to buy an extra round of drinks after the match. Blake wanted all 15 players to be able to take a pass and run with the ball. The tactic could be thrilling—or infuriating. A bout of delicate passing within your own '25' often looked foolhardy. Up in the stand the committee were often on the point of apoplexy. But results justified the audacity.

Bristol's play was based, quite apart from adept handling skill, on a high peak of fitness. The team simply kept running. Opponents were frequently on their knees long before the end. The points tally soared, boosted by the prodigious place-kicking of Cripps. Some people, nurtured on the more dour aspects of conventional rugby, couldn't quite understand what it was all about. Certainly in the early months of the 'revolution' there were rumbles of criticisms.

But the Fifties became known as the Blake Era. There were also more caustic comments about 'misplaced theatre' and 'nancying about the field'. The players chuckled to themselves. No-one could argue with the playing record. Rovers and City had both found a new level; now the rugby players were maintaining the pattern. There had been much to savour—the back row pace of Base, the hooking of Woodward, the sprinting of Ellery, the solidarity of Hazell and Hawkes, Neate, Thorne and Fred Williams, the grit of Blackman and then Redwood.

Now for Bristol's cricketers. The unexploded bombs were cleared from the county ground and the old pros returned under Wally Hammond's leadership in the short term. Most of them looked a trifle more weary about the eyes. They had been away for six years and times were changing. Soon, perish the thought, Gloucestershire would have its first professional captain.

In the immediate post-war years Goddard was still there: with his rather saturnine features, massive hands and distinctive leg-before appeals that umpires thought twice about turning down. There was also a new spinner. 'I'm Cook of Tetbury,' the diffident plumber announced as he reported to Hammond at the pre-season nets. He went into the side, took a wicket with his opening first class delivery, against Oxford, and went on to gobble up 133 in the summer.

Charlie Barnett stayed for a time. He was still prepared to take on the new-ball bowlers, was still reluctant to suffer fools. He left the county more abruptly than anyone expected. His disaffection for Hammond was never too veiled. Wally's own departure had hardly been happy. He was left smarting from the criticism he received during the ill-fated tour of Australia. His declining willingness to communicate to teammates was also a matter of increasing debate.

He had grown old and remote, very different from the extrovert young man who arrived from Cirencester to play for Rovers and court the girls from the Princes when not at the county ground building the foundations of a bountiful career. When he left Gloucestershire, an unscheduled exit, he

Motor racing at Lulsgate in the 1950s.

went to South Africa with his family. He was persuaded to come back on a membership campaign in 1951 and to play one match, against Somerset. It was as embarrassing as it was misplaced. This great, and complex, cricketer was worthy of a better valediction than that.

The winning of the championship had looked a reality in 1947. It was during that season that a friend came to Bristol from deepest Somerset to see his county bat. He checked on the progress of the match, took a stroll around the shops and missed his side altogether. They were bowled out for 25. Goddard took a hat-trick in his 5-4 in three overs. The wicket was viciously libelled and slandered.

Again, in 1959, Gloucestershire went agonisingly close to gaining the title. That was the year when the studious looking John Mortimore completed the double and played in two Test matches. It was also the season when the wrong wicket was prepared at Gloucester for a match against the beguiling Surrey spinners. The result was vital. Lock and Laker won; Gloucestershire lost by 89 runs.

In between these two highly successful summers, Jack Crapp, the quiet Cornishman, become the county's first pro-skipper. He stayed for one year and George Emmett, of the wristy elegance and demeanour of the apparent martinet, for four years. The Graveney brothers had come to make their respective impacts: Tom with his sweet cover-driving grandeur, Ken with his 10 wickets at Chesterfield, an unlikely feat which caused him to say to his teammates: "And I don't believe that bloody spire is crooked, either!"

In addition to Mortimore, both Milton and Allen came from Cotham Grammar School—three boys from the same school, who went on to play for

Whatever the pleasure
Player's complete it

Player's Please

IT'S THE TOBACCO THAT COUNTS

their country. Tony Brown, later to become captain and then secretary-manager, was a product of another grammar school in Bristol, Fairfield. Brown and David Smith opened the bowling together. They were a deceptive pair. The economy of their run-up matched the facility of their control; the record books show the consistency of their performances.

Gloucestershire never completely lacked a sense of humour when George Lambert or Bomber Wells was about. But, alas, cricket was not always a laughing matter for them. WG packed his bags and left in a huff. The farewell of Tom Graveney was anything but felicitous many years later. What did the Sixties hold for the county, initially under the controversial captaincy of the engaging but utterly inexperienced Tom Pugh? Or for Ashton Gate as City dropped back sheepishly into the third division, a fate also in no time at all to befall Rovers?

The artificial fillip of the large crowds immediately after the war hadn't been sustained, either. Professional sport in Bristol was moving into a period of temporary gloom and the irritating old jibe that the West Country 'lacked the stomach' for genuine sporting success could be detected again. It really must have thrown everyone into deep confusion at Eastville and Ashton Gate when Supermac started getting rhetorical and telling us all we'd never had it so good. . .

The Bristol Story

Redcliffe have now published more than 50 books about Bristol. In this we are almost certainly unique both in having produced so many books about a single town, and in dealing with such a wide diversity of aspects.

Indeed, with the possible exception of London, no British town has been as well documented as Bristol.

In our list, you will find several books of personal reminiscence. These are more than exercises in nostalgia. They are tomorrow's history in the making. We have published books, too, on Bristol's rich architectural and artistic heritage, on its famous associations, on the historic harbour and on local industries. With many of these we, and our authors, have worked closely with the City's Museum & Art Gallery or with sponsors, as some of these books could not have been published at popular prices without the enlightened support of local businesses.

In all, Redcliffe have published over one hundred books, from poetry to sport, as well as a strong West Country list. If you would like a copy of our catalogue, please ask.

More Than Just a Good Read

Our White Tree Books imprint provides a service to companies and other organisations interested in book sponsorship.

Sponsoring a book is not a luxury. It's a way of promoting an organisation at remarkably low cost.

It can be used to inform and educate, mark an anniversary, support product publicity, promulgate a cause, aid market identification, reward staff, agent or customer loyalty, or demonstrate community involvement.

If you have something to celebrate or a story to tell—or simply want to know how sponsorship could work for you—please give us a call on Bristol (0272) 290158. Or write—White Tree Books, 49 Park Street, Bristol BS1 5NT.